THE

ECLECTIC

PROGRESSIVE SPELLING BOOK.

ON AN IMPROVED PLAN:

SHOWING THE EXACT SOUND OF EACH SYLLABLE,
ACCORDING TO THE MOST APPROVED
PRINCIPLES OF

ENGLISH ORTHOEPY.

DESIGNED TO PRECEDE

THE ECLECTIC READERS.

By
ALEXANDER H. McGUFFEY,

— 1838 —

CINCINNATI:
PUBLISHED BY TRUMAN AND SMITH.
150 MAIN STREET

ROMAN NUMERALS EXPLAINED.

A numeral is a symbol meaning number. Our system of counting is believed to have begun by people counting on their fingers. Both the Arabic (1, 2, 3, 4, etc.) and the Roman (I, II, III, IV, etc.) are believed to have started this way. The word digit, meaning number, is from the Latin word digitus, meaning finger. The number V (5) seems to be representative of an open hand; and, the number X (10) seems to be like two open hands.

In earlier days, our forefathers used the Roman system to indicate chapter headings in books. To help you understand those numbers more easily you may refer to the chart below:

Roman	Arabic	Roman	Arabic	Roman	Arabic
I	1	XI	11	XXX	30
II	2	XII	12	XL	40
III	3	XIII	13	L	50
IV	4	XIV	14	LX	60
V	5	XV	15	LXX	70
VI	6	XVI	16	LXXX	80
VII	7	XVII	17	XC	90
VIII	8	XVIII	18	C	100
IX	9	XIX	19	D	500
X	10	XX	20	M	1000

Entered according to Act of Congress, in the year 1838
By TRUMAN & SMITH,
In the Clerk's Office for the District Court of Ohio.

The Original McGuffey's ™ is a trade-mark of Mott Media, Inc.

This edition copyright © 1982 by Mott Media, Inc., 1000 East Huron Street, Milford, Michigan 48042

Robert Burkett, Editor

ISBN 0-88062-000-5
Printed in the United States of America

PRESENT PUBLISHER'S PREFACE.

Alexander Hamilton McGuffey, younger brother of William Holmes McGuffey, was a integral part of much of the writing of the *original* Eclectic Readers. His contribution of the Eclectic Speller and the Fifth Reader, (*Rhetorical Guide*), greatly enhanced the thoroughness of these educational tools.

Millions of copies of these early textbooks were sold in their *original* Christ-centered form. The character of our Nation was molded in an upright manner through the repeated use of these textbooks over several generations.

In order to capture the true spirit of the *original* McGuffey's Eclectic Readers we have made no major content changes. While this edition of the *authentic* Eclectic Progressive Spelling Book is being presented in a more easily readable form, the stories, poems, and pictures appear as they did in the first edition.

Slight changes have taken place for the sake of clarification. Those changes are as follows: a. on page 27 and 28 the last half of the lessons are missing in the original edition so it was necessary to fill in spelling words which seemed appropriate; b. on page 39 the last sentence was added for sake of clarification.

The Publisher wishes to express his heart-felt appreciation to the staff of the Special Collections Library at Miami University, Oxford, Ohio, for its cooperation in researching the *authenticity* of this book. Additionally, we desire to thank Dr. John H. Westerhoff, III, for his inspiration in promoting the republishing of the *original* works and Bohn Printing for their untiring efforts in typesetting the Readers.

It is indeed an honor and distinct pleasure to return the *original* McGuffey's Eclectic Readers to you. The content of this series will help you develop outstanding reading skills, Christ-centered character, a love for good literature, and impressive speaking abilities. I am sure you will find the *original* McGuffey's Eclectic Readers to be a valuable teaching tool whether they are used in the public school, Christian school, or for those who choose to teach their children at home.

George M. Mott, President
MOTT MEDIA, INC.

PREFACE.

In the preparation of this book, it has been the author's aim to avoid complexity of plan, as far as possible. Hence it will be observed that he has simplified the ordinary vowel sounds. The difference between the sound of *o* in *nor* and *not*; of *a* in *fall* and *wad*, as well as between *u* in *rule* and *tube*, seems too nice to be appreciated by an unpractised ear. These distinctions being unnecessary, and tending only to embarrass the learner, have not been retained.

In the orthography of such words as *music, public*, &c. formerly terminating with *ck*;—and in *favor, honor*, &c. formerly spelled *our*, the *k* and *u* are omitted, agreeably to the principles of Dr. Webster, whose philological labors entitle him to the gratitude of every American.

The reading lessons, most of which are new, have been progressively arranged; and it is hoped they will be found both interesting and instructive.

ENTERED according to Act of Congress,
in the year 1838,
BY TRUMAN AND SMITH,
In the Clerk's Office for the District Court of Ohio.

Sterotyped by
GLEZEN AND SHEPARD,
29 Pearl St., Cincinnati.

ANALYSIS
OF
THE ENGLISH ALPHABET.

LETTERS are characters made to represent sounds. Syllables are formed of letters; words are formed of syllables. There are twenty-six letters in the English language, namely: A, B, C, D, E, F, G, H, I, J, K ,L ,M, N, O, P, Q, R, S, T, U, V, W, X, Y, Z. These letters taken together are called the English Alphabet.

The ALPHABET is divided into VOWELS and CONSONANTS. A VOWEL is a letter which can be sounded by itself, without the use of another letter.

The VOWELS are A, E, I, O, U, W; Y is sometimes a vowel and sometimes a consonant.

NOTE.—It has been customary to consider W a consonant when it commences a word; but Dr. Webster, with apparent reason, claims that it is always a vowel. It surely answers the usual definition of a vowel, viz: "a letter which can be sounded by itself;" and agrees closely in pronunciation with the OU of the French, and the U of the Spanish.

The CONSONANTS are B, C, D, F, G, H, J, K, L, M, N, P, Q, R, S, T, V, X, Z, and sometimes Y.

QUESTIONS. What do letters represent? Of what are syllables formed? How many letters are there in the English alphabet? What are they? How is the alphabet divided? What is a vowel? Repeat the vowels. Repeat the consonants. What letter is both a vowel and a consonant?

DIPHTHONGS AND TRIPHTHONGS.
In every syllable there must be at least one vowel. When two vowels are united in one sound, so as to

form one syllable, their union is called a diphthong; as OU in *loud*; EA in *ea-ger*.

The union of three vowels in one syllable it called a triphthong; as IEU in *lieu*.

A *pure* diphthong is one in which the sounds of both vowels are united; as OI in *voice, oil*.

An *impure* diphthong is one in which one of the vowels only is sounded; as AI in *aim*.

There are four pure diphthongs; OI, OY, OU, and OW; as in *toil, boy, round, cow*; OU and OW are sometimes impure, as in *tough, low*.

The impure diphthongs in common use, are AE, AI, AU, AW, AY, EA, EI, EO, EU, EW, EY, IA, IE, OA, OE, OO, UA, UE, UI: as in *seal, autumn, coal, bread, sail, say, either, yeoman, people,* &c.

QUESTIONS. What is a diphthong? A triphthong? What is a pure diphthong? An impure diphthong? Give examples of words in which there are pure diphthongs. Give examples of words in which there are impure diphthongs. Give examples of triphthongs.

SOUNDS OF THE VOWELS.

A has four sounds; lst, a long sound, as in f$\overset{1}{a}$te; 2d, a flat sound, as in f$\overset{2}{a}$r; 3d, a broad sound, as in f$\overset{3}{a}$ll, wh$\overset{3}{a}$t; 4th, a short sound, as in f$\overset{4}{a}$t.

NOTE.—The difference between the sounds of A in *fall* and *what*, are deemed too nice to be appreciated by an unpracticed ear, and therefore no distinction has been made between them in this table. The same thing may be said with regard to the sounds of O in *nor* and *not*; and of U, in *rule* and *tube*.

G has two sounds; hard, as in *gave*; soft, as in *ģem*. When marked with the cedilla (ģ), it is soft.

H is but a forcible breathing before the following vowel. It is silent after R, as in *rhyme*. When preceded by W. it is sounded before it, as in *when*, (pronounced *hwen*.)

J has the sound of G soft, as in *Jane*. In *hallelujah*, it takes the sound of Y.

K has but one sound, as in *kind*.

L has one sound, as in *live*. It is often silent when followed by another consonant, as in *calm*.

M, N, P, Q and R have one sound each, as in *man*, *not*, *pit*, *question*, *run*. Q is always followed by U; *together, they are pronounced like KW, as in quite*, pronounced *kwite*.

S has a soft sound, as in *set*, and the sound of Z, as in *rise*. When marked with a cedilla (ş) it has the sound of Z.

T and V have one sound each, as in *tin*, *vice*.

X has the sound of KS, as in *wax*; and of GS, as in *exact*; and of Z, as in *Xenophon*.

Y and Z have one sound each, as in *yes*, *zinc*.

QUESTIONS. How are consonants divided? What are mutes? Name them. What are semi-vowels? Name them. What are liquids? Name them.

NOTE.—The teacher will find it highly advantageous to question the pupil *minutely* and *carefully*, on the above table of consonant sounds, calling for examples, &c.

DOUBLE CONSONANTS.

Ch have the sound nearly of *tsh*, as in *church*; of *k*, as in *chorus*, and of *sh*, as in *chaise*.

Gh are generally mute; when pronounced, they take the sound of G hard, as in *ghost*, or of F, as in *tough*.

Ph have the sound of F, as in *philosophy*.

Sh have but one sound, as in *ship*.

Th have an aspirate sound, as in *think*; or hard, as in *thou*.

QUESTIONS. What is the sound of Ch? Of Gh? Of Ph? Of Sh? Of Th?

FINAL SYLLABLES.

The final syllables *cean, cion, sion, tion,* have the sound of *shun*[2], as in *ocean, suspicion, version, commotion.*

Ceous, cious, scious, tious, have the sound of *shus*[2]; as in *cetaceous, gracious, conscious, cautious.*

Cian, tian, have the sound of *shan*[4], as in *magician, gentian.*

Cial, sial, tial, have the sound of *shl*[a], as in *social, ambrosial, partial.*

Science, tience, have the sound of *shense*[2], as in *conscience, patience.*

QUESTIONS. What is the sound of the final syllables, *cean, cion, sion, tion?* Give examples. What is the sound of *ceous, cious, scious, tious?* Of *cian, tian?* Of *cial, sial, tial?* Of *science, tience?* Give examples of each of the above.

REVIEW.

Repeat the letters of the Alphabet. How is the Alphabet divided? How many vowels are there? What are they? What letter is both a vowel and a consonant? What do you call the union of two vowels in one syllable? What the union of three vowels? Repeat the table of the vowel sounds, and give examples. What are mutes? Repeat them. What are semi-vowels? What are liquids? What are some of the double consonants, and how are they sounded? Can you give examples of the irregular sounds of the vowels?

ALPHABET.

A	a	*A*	*a*	L	l
B	b	*B*	*b*	P	p
C	c	*C*	*c*	N	n
D	d	*D*	*d*	R	r
E	e	*E*	*e*	Z	z
F	f	*F*	*f*	Q	q
G	g	*G*	*g*	M	m
H	h	*H*	*h*	Y	y
I	i	*I*	*i*	K	k
J	j	*J*	*j*	C	c
K	k	*K*	*k*	J	j
L	l	*L*	*l*	F	f
M	m	*M*	*m*	B	b
N	n	*N*	*n*	U	u
O	o	*O*	*o*	A	a
P	p	*P*	*p*	G	g
Q	q	*Q*	*q*	E	e
R	r	*R*	*r*	X	x
S	s	*S*	*s*	D	d
T	t	*T*	*t*	W	w
U	u	*U*	*u*	S	s
V	v	*V*	*v*	I	i
W	w	*W*	*w*	T	t
X	x	*X*	*x*	V	v
Y	y	*Y*	*y*	O	o
Z	z	*Z*	*z*	H	h

| 1 | 2 | 3 | 4 | 1 | 2 | 1 | 2 | 1 | 2 |
fate, far, fall, fat,—me, met,—pine, pin,—no, move

SECTION I.

Syllables of two letters, beginning with a consonant.

1	1	1	1	1	1
ba	be	bi	bo	bu	by
da	de	di	do	du	dy
fa	fe	fi	fo	fu	fy
ha	he	hi	ho	hu	hy

1	1	1	1	1	1
ka	ke	ki	ko	ku	ky
la	le	li	lo	lu	ly
ma	me	mi	mo	mu	my
na	ne	ni	no	nu	ny

1	1	1	1	1	1
pa	pe	pi	po	pu	py
ra	re	ri	ro	ru	ry
sa	se	si	so	su	sy
ta	te	ti	to	tu	ty

1	1	1	1	1	1
va	ve	vi	vo	vu	vy
ba	ke	ti	ro	nu	ny
za	ze	zi	zo	zu	zy
wa	we	wi	wo	wu	wy

1	1	1	1	1	1
fu	ga	ra	ku	dy	za
fe	he	ru	ki	do	li
fy	ho	ri	ke	de	sa
fo	hu	ro	ko	di	zu

SECTION II.

Syllables of two letters, beginning with a vowel.

4	2	2	3	2
ab	eb	ib	ob	ub
ac	ec	ic	oc	uc
ad	ed	id	od	ud
af	ef	if	of	uf

4	2	2	3	2
ag	eg	ig	og	ug
al	el	il	ol	ul
am	em	im	om	um
an	en	in	on	un

4	2	2	3	2
ap	ep	ip	op	up
as	es	is	os	us
ax	ex	ix	ox	ux
ar	er	ir	or	ur

4	2	2	3	2
ak	ek	ik	ok	uk
az	ez	iz	oz	uz
at	et	it	ot	ut
av	ev	iv	ov	uv

4	2	2	3	2
ag	en	ur	of	if
ad	im	ex	ox	uf
as	ul	it	on	ef
an	ne	ep	os	id

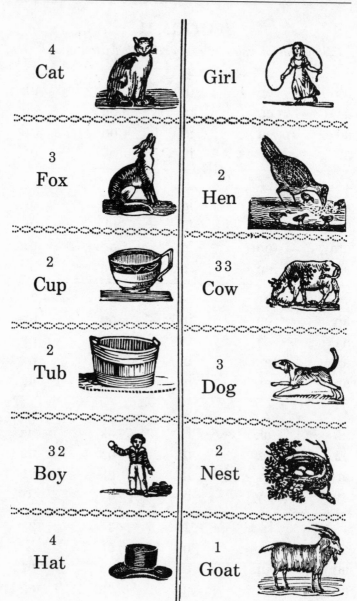

4
Cat

Girl

3
Fox

2
Hen

2
Cup

3 3
Cow

2
Tub

3
Dog

3 2
Boy

2
Nest

4
Hat

1
Goat

3　　4　　　1　　　2　　　3　　32　33
nor, good,—tube, tub, bull,—oil, pound,—thin, THIS

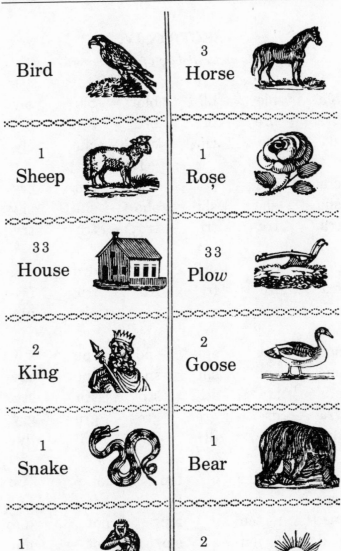

Bird

3
Horse

1
Sheep

1
Roṣe

33
House

33
Plow

2
King

2
Goose

1
Snake

1
Bear

1
Ape

2
Sun

1	2	3	4	1	2	1	2	1	2
fate,	far,	fall,	fat,—	me,	met,—	pine,	pin,—	no,	move

SECTION IV.

Words and syllables of three letters.

1	1	1	1	1	1
bla	ble	bli	blo	blu	bly
bra	bre	bri	bro	bru	bry
cla	cle	cli	clo	clu	cly

1	1	1	1	1	1
cra	cre	cri	cro	cru	cry
sha	she	shi	sho	shu	shy
tra	tre	tri	tro	tru	try

1	1	1	1	1	1
dra	dre	dri	dro	dru	dry
fra	fre	fri	fro	fru	fry
pla	ple	pli	plo	plu	ply

1	1	1	1	1	1
spa	spe	spi	spo	spu	spy
sna	sne	sni	sno	snu	sny
sta	ste	sti	sto	stu	sty
gra	gre	gri	gro	gru	gry
fla	fle	fli	flo	flu	fly

4	2	2	3	2
bad	den	hip	lot	tub
lad	men	lip	hot	hub
mad	ten	nip	not	dub
pad	fen	sip	pot	nut
rat	hen	sit	got	rut
fan	net	sin	rot	run
tax	set	six	hop	sun

3	4	1	2	3	32	33

nor, good,—tube, tub, bull,—oil, pound,—thin, THIS

4	2	2	3	2
sap	let	nil	dog	sup
nap	hem	lit	don	jut
hat	fed	kid	dot	rug
lad	leg	mit	pop	sum
ban	pet	fit	top	lug
2	**3**	**4**	**1**	**2**
far	not	fat	ape	keg
mar	war	bat	dry	fen
met	top	pan	old	mix
ten	for	hat	uşe	rig
pin	sop	fan	fry	his
pig	raw	rat	try	hum
tub	fox	hag	cry	hut
2	**3**	**4**	**1**	**1**
pun	law	gap	sty	ray
pug	cot	cat	eve	day
tun	hop	lag	ire	she
rum	saw	sad	içe	vie
tar	maw	fan	ode	tie
par	pod	dam	ore	doe
2	**3**	**4**	**1**	**1**
pet	rot	mat	fly	pry
sit	sot	map	shy	sky
tip	paw	rag	ope	dry
jar	caw	tax	age	hay
bar	daw	lap	açe	may
car	wan	man	ale	lay

1	2	3	4	1	2	1	2	1	2

fate, far, fall, fat,—me, met,—pine, pin,—no, move

2	3	2	1	4
rim	dot	art	nay	sap
net	*waş	ark	say	tan
mug	ja*w*	den	gay	sat
let	got	car	ray	aft
bud	lop	wet	day	apt
sun	mop	par	pay	tap

SECTION V.

Words of four letters.

1	1	2	2	3
rate	bone	part	tush	halt
make	hole	carp	rust	warm
rare	hope	cart	sunk	bald
save	note	harp	must	sort
tame	rude	tart	dust	plot
lave	roşe	lark	dusk	full
rape	tube	barn	hulk	pull
gate	tune	mart	lung	lord
take	mute	park	bung	halt

1	1	2	2	3
wave	muşe	nest	curl	stop
wane	cake	less	gust	horn
line	life	test	gush	malt
time	cove	felt	cart	morn
vine	cure	west	hard	shot

* Letters marked with a cedilla (,) have a soft sound.

3	4	1	2	3	32	33

nor, good,—tube, tub, bull,—oil, pound,—thin, THIS

1	1	2	2	4
wine	cane	went	gush	mast
like	fine	rent	tell	pant
lime	cave	tent	gift	fast
nine	noşe	desk	tush	rasp
niçe	duke	self	lift	gasp
side	hive	left	melt	hang
tire	post	gilt	sent	task
pine	bolt	trip	bent	flat
pipe	fort	lift	hurt	cram
mote	lake	hilt	hurl	trap

1	1	2	2	4
more	vane	sing	silk	mash
hove	lone	hunt	sift	slap
rote	roşe	link	thin	tank
rove	post	king	pent	snap
rope	dolt	gild	hark	hash
sore	mule	tilt	dent	dash

2	1	2	4	1
carp	time	drum	lash	bole
skin	here	smut	cask	rove
quit	bind	snug	snap	pole
rich	bolt	less	trap	pope
hint	wane	drug	rank	lute
fern	riçe	nest	rang	rude
sent	tire	lent	raft	tune
sill	rule	hemp	cash	cure

1	2	3	4	1	2	1	2	1	2
fate,	far,	fall,	fat,—me,	met,—pine,	pin,—no,	move

2	1	2	4	1
lump	tile	mint	cram	joke
turn	yoke	self	trap	core
hurt	feel	silk	span	vote
slit	sore	lint	slap	dote
slip	seen	fish	spat	cube
crib	teem	chip	mash	dole
sing	dare	disk	lack	riçe
trip	cove	dish	rant	dome
chub	hare	hush	rasp	fife
mush	mane	hulk	sash	sine

2	1	2	4	1
fill	lake	husk	damp	tore
till	lane	hull	bank	lure
hull	sake	loop	lamp	mute
cull	fate	soot	camp	pore
null	vile	surd	dash	mote
dull	hate	ship	wrap	bile
fell	wade	tilt	clan	ripe
sell	seer	gulf	clam	dive
tell	pate	mood	dram	miçe
bell	save	rift	sham	rode

2	1	2	4	1
soon	sane	buzz	look	fuçe
moon	vane	clip	mast	mole
moot	riçe	bent	soot	tile
turk	ripe	wish	took	sale
lump	cove	tent	past	mere

| 3 | 4 | 1 | 2 | 3 | 32 | 33 |
nor, good,—tube, tub, bull,—oil, pound,—thin, THIS

SECTION VI.

Words of two syllables, accented on the first.

1 4	1 2	1 2	2 2
ru' ral	di' et	plo' ver	ev' er
di al	ho ly	pro em	en ter
fi nal	on ly	ta per	in to
bru tal	ju ry	tu mid	ug ly
re al	va ry	qui et	bil let
cli max	pu ny	vo ter	bit ter
fi at	ra çy	wa fer	bel fry

1 4	1 2	1 2	2 2
ri val	ba sis	to per	bet ter
du cal	cri sis	tu lip	çiv et
du cat	no ted	wa fer	çiv il
mu ral	la dy	na ked	clev er
lu nar	ta ken	na dir	crit ic
na tal	o ver	cu bic	fen nel
pa gan	e vil	mu sic	fet ter
ve nal	po em	ti ler	ex it

1 4	1 2	1 2	2 2
vi al	po tent	ti dy	fif ty
plu ral	pu pil	ro py	per il
pa pal	fu my	na vy	ep ic
sa tan	ru by	ro ver	cut ler
pe tal	po ker	go ing	fus tic
lo cal	re bus	pa per	fun nel
vi tal	sha dy	ra ted	riv er

1	2	3	4	1	2	1	2	1	2
fate,	far,	fall,	fat,—me,		met,—pine,		pin,—no,		move

1 4	1 2	1 2	2 2
vo' cal	to' ry	mu' sic	cut' ler
tri al	i çy	le gal	din ner
hu man	i vy	tri al	pil fer
va cant	mi ry	gra vy	jes ter
to tal	va ry	ha ted	hus ky
bi as	o men	ta ker	hun ter

2 2	2 2	4 2	4 2
fet ter	kit ten	al um	ash es
let ter	lim it	am ber	ad it
fend er	lin en	ax is	asp en
bet ter	pep per	rab bit	bar rel
dip per	pip pin	pal lid	car ry
cur rent	per ry	tat ter	dap per
ar my	mit ten	tam per	fab ric
liv id	mut ter	lap pet	gam ut
mar tin	test y	sam ple	mal let

2 2	2 2	4 2	4 2
hil ly	tes ter	tan ner	nap kin
gul let	ten nis	cab in	man ly
gin ger	tur nip	pat ent	lat tiçe
mud dy	net tle	tab let	lad der
hec tic	nib ble	stam mer	rab id
çiv il	mem ber	gan der	ral ly
gun ner	rus tic	bas ket	pat ter
dul çet	pig gin	bat ter	plat ter
dex ter	wel kin	man ner	jas per
lit tle	reb el	lat ter	clap per

3   4   1   2   3   32 33
nor, good,—tube, tub, bull,—oil, pound,—thin, THIS

2 2	2 2	4 2	4 2
hel' met	sin' ner	lan' çet	cran' ny
gid dy	sul len	tap ster	clas sic
gus set	seg ment	cav ern	dan çer
in step	sim per	ant ler	gar ret
cul prit	lit ter	hat ter	raf ter
ful çent	lar der	ham mer	ham per
nut meg	pun çent	tav ern	hab it

2 2	2 2	4 2	4 2
cum ber	riv et	ban ner	ham let
viv id	cur rent	hap pen	hap pen
frit ter	rud dy	an tic	pal lid
clus ter	sun set	ban dit	nap kin
sil ly	pend ent	ad it	ram ble
ver min	sum mit	can dy	rap id
pup py	rug ged	an vil	rat tle

2 1	3 2	1	2
in nate	or bit	li on	fel on
jun to	sor did	fu el	un der
rav age	cor net	pi per	mer it
ter raçe	tor pid	pi lot	pil fer
tes tate	slop py	va cate	win dy
viş age	sol id	na tal	dul çet
vul gate	dol lar	sa cred	mur der
em pire	ton ic	va cant	hun ter
wel fare	ful ly	se cret	run let
ex port	vom it	fe male	arm ful
im port	pul pit	ba con	car pet

1	2	3	4	1	2	1	2	1	2
fate, far, fall, fat,—me, met,—pine, pin,—no, move

2 1	3 2	1	2
sen' ate	top' ic	ha' zel	cast' ing
pres to	tor rent	do tard	man ly
dic tate	vor tex	dro nish	car rot
um pire	fall en	gru el	bit ter
kim bo	tor ment	du el	nib ble
six teen	call ing	i ron	tip pler
trib ute	hor net	mi ner	mix ture
lim bo	for ty	ne gus	nec tar
mid way	lord ly	za ny	bat ten

2 1	3 2	1	2
ut most	stop per	wa ry	car ry
ef fort	fal ter	ca per	mas sive
con trite	morn ing	çi der	tax ing
in mate	halt er	fu ming	rend ing
lux ate	bon net	rue ful	tempt er
trun cate	full er	na sal	cup ping
stag nate	bul let	pe tal	wiz ard
pal açe		a corn	nar rate

SECTION VII.

Words of two syllables, accented on the second.

4 2	1 1	1 1	1 2
ad mit'	re ly'	ju ly'	re mit'
an nul	re pine	be side	be set
as sist	se cure	de bate	re fer
a bet	de duçe	be hind	re bel
ad just	de cree	cre ate	mo lest

| 3 | 4 | 1 | 2 | 3 | 32 | 33 |
nor, good,—tube, tub, bull,—oil, pound,—thin, THIS

4 2	1 1	1 1	1 2
an nex'	de face'	de lude'	re pel'
ar rest	fore go	di late	o mit
at tend	be hind	de fy	di ġest
a mid	e rase	be take	co erçe
ac quit	pre çede	be have	re move
a lert	re vile	re take	re mit
a far	re gale	se rene	ro bust
ap prove	de laẏ	de mure	re vent
a do	de vote	e voke	re fer

4 2	1 1	1 1	1 2
a loof	se date	re plaçe	re fund
ca det	re tire	be hold	de fer
ca ress	re voke	re port	de bar
a miss	u nite	e lope	su perb
ad vert	pro çeed	re ply	ho tel
a larm	su preme	re told	e vinçe
a verse	de fame	re çede	se lect
as sert	de gree	re vere	de duct
ad just	re pute	pro fane	e rect

2 1	2 1	2 2	4 4
en tire	in voke	dis till	a las
sa lute	un safe	ex pel	a mass
en roll	ob scure	un til	a baft
ex clude	man kind	em bark	ca nal
ex pire	par take	in fer	at tract
di vide	in trude	un bar	rat an
in quire	mi nute	in ert	cra vat

| 1 | 2 | 3 | 4 | 1 | 2 | 1 | 2 | 1 | 2 |
fate, far, fall, fat,—me, met,—pine, pin,—no, move

2 1	2 1	2 2	4 4
ex çite'	in duçe'	in sist'	trans act'
en robe	dis play	sub sist	a bash
dis uşe	set tee	in tent	a back
il lude	un seen	per plex	gal lant
in ure	un fold	in cur	a far
dis may	un lade	per mit	a mass

2 1	3 1	2 2	1 2
em pale	con trol	en rich	re mit
en gage	con sume	ef fect	re pel
im bibe	col late	dis pel	de bar
in hale	com bine	im pel	re şent
en grave	com mune	neg lect	be set
in vade	con trive	per turb	se lect
en case	con fute	un fix	be fit
ef façe	con voke	ex tend	re miss
ter rene	con nive	up held	re mark
dis pute	com poşe	sub mit	re gret
in sane	com pile	ex tend	o mit
im ply	con jure	dis miss	re lax

2 1	3 1	2 2	1 2
es cape	con spire	mis give	pro tect
dis creet	com ply	dis card	ro bust
in deed	pol lute	ex pert	e mit
im port	cor rode	ex pel	e lect
un lade	con fine	per vert	re fund
un ripe	com plete	in ject	u surp
sur vive	con çede	in sist	be deck

| 3 | 4 | 1 | 2 | 3 | 32 | 33 |
nor, good,—tube, tub, bull,—oil, pound,—thin, THIS

1 4	1 4	1 4	4 4
se dan'	re lax'	be gan'	a las'
de vast	re plant	de cant	a bash
re past	de camp	co act	a far
tre pan	re pass	re act	ca nal

SECTION VIII.

Monosyllables of five letters.

1	1	1	1	1
crape	spume	triçe	creek	truçe
waste	plume	while	prive	prude
drake	prune	gripe	pride	grape
plate	blade	cloşe	droll	teeth
paste	glide	prime	stove	sheep
haste	globe	sport	shorn	sheer
glade	probe	stove	proşe	blame
fleet	glebe	white	sloth	beech
creep	tribe	brine	chase	steer

1	1	1	1	1
cheer	spade	speed	chafe	grind
greet	traçe	grime	queen	shorn
check	sliçe	scare	sweet	queer
pride	spike	flute	steed	stove
trite	crude	green	troll	swine
snipe	prude	shave	forth	spine
twill	choke	tripe	sport	spaçe
smell	frame	theme	taste	state
space	slime	creed	forge	chafe

1	2	3	4	1	2	1	2	1	2
fate,	far,	fall,	fat,—	me,	met,—	pine,	pin,—	no,	move

1	1	1	1	1
chine	smile	snore	shase	sleet
spire	prate	sleet	probe	speed
grope	bride	sleep	slope	three
prone	snake	whale	grace	grave
store	spoke	forge	porch	shave
slope	clime	prose	prate	score
grind	swine	stone	sheer	spike
trope	slide	spire	skate	stage
smoke	grade	grove	spare	gross

2	2	2	4
charm	shark	strip	craft
scarf	smart	think	gland
barge	larch	crush	grant
harsh	stark	fresh	clash
chest	blend	hençe	clank
cleft	spend	print	shaft
dense	terse	hinge	plant
shelf	verse	singe	clang

2	2	2	4
drill	hençe	fling	shalt
sharp	sprig	stint	flask
float	bring	pençe	crash
frill	blink	flint	clasp
sting	chink	fudge	glass
drank	drink	spilt	stamp
blimp	brood	stilt	staffs
brush	broom	plump	stand

| 3 | 4 | 1 | 2 | 3 | 32 | 33 |

nor, good,—tube, tub, bull,—oil, pound,—thin, THIS

2	2	2	4
cluck	shoot	stoop	slash
stump	bloom	troop	shook
crust	stool	sloop	crook
prove	goose	trust	brook
groom	clung	curds	grand
sloop	gruff	carts	grasp
stool	trunk	winds	glass
spoon	pluck	fresh	stood
chart	strut	flint	plash
cress	clump	chest	smash
blest	parse	parts	stand
crisp	surge	dress	grass
grist	roost	drink	trick
troop	smell	smelt	chime
spurn	shift	think	start

SECTION IX.

Words of two syllables, accented on the first.

2 2	2 2	2 2	1 2
car' pet	par' ent	con' vent	re' run
fen nel	per fect	lum ber	no tice
tem per	per jure	for mer	bed lam
tat tler	in fant	won der	se cret
tin ner	sim ple	per son	spi der
turn er	pres ent	in jure	be ing
mem ber	win ter	cap tive	fe ver
com et	wel come	mas ter	an gel

1	2	3	4	1	2	1	2	1	2

fate, far, fall, fat,—me, met,—pine, pin,—no, move

2 2	2 2	2 2	2 2
mut' ter	nut' meg	part' ing	mer' it
sul len	rub ber	sip ping	thun der
num ber	flesh y	mer it	min strel
gar ret	gar nish	bur ġess	splin ter
gar den	in flux	dit ty	dif fer
mar ket	rel ict	plen ty	shiv er
farm er	cun ning	ca ter	cur vet
start er	cur rent	clar et	mus ket
near est	sig net	vest ry	nut shell

2 2	2 2	2 2	2 2
wa ter	sil ly	trink et	harp er
gen tle	sim per	skil let	ġin ġer
wag on	ten der	sput ter	trip ping
hun ger	sur face	viṣ it	spar ring
far mer	par don	wind mill	skip per
un der	ser vant	vint ner	mix ing
for est	aw ful	sil ver	min im
vis it	**mag** ic	fil bert	pig ment
fin ger	han dle	an ger	pen guin

1 2	2 1	2 1	2
o dor	sur plus	ar my	ter ror
dan ger	com bine	hon ey	tem per
fro zen	win dow	mon key	rig or
mo ment	six teen	a pex	shil ling
pre view	tis sue	in ner	er ror
pre text	ar gues	al ways	pen cil
be ing	Sun day	fif teen	tur tle

3	4	1	2	3	32	33

nor, good,—tube, tub, bull,—oil, pound,—thin, THIS

2 2	3 2	1 3	2 2
link' ing	sort' ment	waste' ful	hil' lock
fool ish	fall ing	co lon	ren der
cool ing	storm y	ri ot	set tle
fen çing	form ing	graçe ful	pis tol
spir it	for çeps	tu tor	piv ot
pert ness	short ness	stu por	sim per
pep per	ful ly	care ful	art ful
sul phur	good ness	tune ful	hum ble
prin çess	full ness	wo ful	car go
print er	salt ing	li on	but ter
miz zen	tor pid	hope ful	bar ber
boor ish	vor tex	pi lot	car ver
par tridge	hor net	rue ful	bar ter
stuf fing	hor rid	hope ful	cur rent

2 2	3 2	2 1	2 2
sys tem	top ple	whet stone	stut ter
vul gar	mor tar	mem brane	ten nis
ren net	bor der	brim stone	nes tle
spell ing	rot ten	pin case	ten don
ship ment	pock et	in mate	ar mor
sling er	pot ter	pil low	er ror
trump et	tor rent	min now	sym bol
slen der	morn ing	del uge	ped ler
spin et	tall er	lev ee	spig ot
dim ple	bul let	in jure	good ly
rob in	short en	ref use	mis sive

1	2	3	4	1	2	1	2	1	2
fate,	far,	fall,	fat,—	me,	met,—	pine,	pin,—	no,	move

SECTION X.

Monosyllables of three or more letters, containing
diphthongs, and silent letters.

1	1	1	1	1
aim	air	içe	load	oak
bay	tea	age	ear	eel
sue	tie	way	pea	own
sea	vie	die	hoe	say
jay	way	nay	pay	owe

1	1	1	1	1
mew	the	dear	yea	oats
bait	deal	each	coal	coax
knee	high	hoar	know	leaf
lewd	loam	sigh	soak	knoll
soap	foam	year	maid	peat

2	2	2	32	32
dumb	earl	gape	coy	troy
soup	palm	neck	oil	cloy
move	tick	who	doit	hoy
urge	kick	luck	boil	loin
alms	dead	lead	foil	join
head	lead	deaf	coit	soil
limb	bread	aunt	toil	toy
calm	earn	tour	boy	joy

3	3	3	3	33
paw	daw	caul	laud	bout
lock	awl	awe	mock	out
claw	walk	jaw	stock	rout

3	4	1	2	3	32	33

nor, good,—tube, tub, bull,—oil, pound,—thin, THIS

3	3	3	3	33
hawk	maw	lawn	pock	owl
dock	knob	sock	call	noun
saw	haul	rock	calk	cowl

1	1	1	1	1
beak	both	ache	hew	coat
boar	sigh	isle	flue	four
jail	lain	fain	knew	know
meat	fair	heat	heap	eaşe
loaf	flea	high	nail	pair

1	1	1	1	1
die	high	night	nigh	right
sign	gaol	sight	light	light
seal	seam	seem	seat	team
treat	zeal	year	yield	climb
dight	bloat	ghost	snow	soak
road	roar	plight	coach	float
leaf	ream	rear	neap	thee
plea	flea	peak	maim	main

1	1	1	1	1
vail	tier	ideş	wear	pier
lead	weak	hear	veal	view
oath	tear	tear	soul	plea
stay	play	plain	knave	steak
mail	maize	vail	waist	straight
bewail	brief	freak	key	nieçe
please	base	fiend	creak	creep
crease	gear	least	heat	chief

1	2	3	4	1	2	1	2	1	2
fate,	far,	fall,	fat,—	me,	met,—	pine,	pin,—	no,	move

SECTION XI.

Words of two syllables accented on the first; containing diphthongs and silent letters.

Note.—Progressive reading lessons are added to each page, in the following Sections.

1	2	1	2	1	2	1	2
say' ing		sea' son		trea' ty		grea' şy	
dea con		oak um		year ly		neat ly	
migh t y		fair ly		ea şy		near ly	
fai ry		wea ry		safe guard		jail er	
la den		man ger		pha sis		gai ly	
aid ing		claim er		cai tiff		bail iff	
gait ers		clay ish		ail ment		dain ty	
niçe ly		nine ty		dai şy		ne gus	
fa mous		mould y		low ly		se rous	

1	2	1	2	1	2	1	2
read er		paint ing		mean ly		may or	
hoa ry		hu man		neat ness		oat en	
jail er		play er		po rous		peo ple	
sneak ing		migh t y		mea ger		leak y	
ligh t en		jui çy		pa tience		neu tral	
poul tiçe		stain ing		wea şel		hea then	
wri ting		wri ter		rea şon		priest ly	
weak ness		shoul der		thiev ish		sci ence	

My top is in a tin box.   The rat is in a hole.
Go and get the lid.   Puss can not get him.
Let us shut it up.   Do not come out old
Now the lid is on.   rat.

3　4　1　2　3　32　33
nor, good,—tube, tub, bull,—oil, pound,—thin, THIS

1	2	1	2	2	2	2	2
cam' bric	rain' y	sick' ly	lep' rous
frail ty	trea cle	çer tain	heart y
fright en	stream er	nour ish	zeal ous
gain er	stran ger	heart less	vil lain
fa mous	nail er	guilt y	çur tain
fight ing	great er	bar gain	dead ly
court ly	speak ing	dead en	feath er
dea con	weav er	friend less	heav en
deal ing	leap ing	friend ly	heav y

2	2	2	2	2	2	2	2
head y	deaf ness	deaf en	coun try
clean ly	cleanş ing	leath er	vaunt ing
pearl y	health ful	health y	calm ly
peaş ant	pleaş ant	head long	flour ish
friend ship	treaş ure	neaş ure	huck ster
couş in	vaunt ed	check er	isth mus
calm ness	dis tich	bis cuit	ker chief
leop ard	fa ther	tempt er	troub le
young ster	vis cous	Thurş day	tur key

The fox has a den.
I saw him dig it.
I was on the hill.
We shot off a gun.
The fox ran out.
His fur was red.
We sat on a tree.

The snow is cold.
The sun is warm.
The fire is hot.
Keep out of harm.
We see by a lamp.
Do not put it out.
You and I will go.

1	2	3	4	1	2	1	2	1	2
fate,	far,	fall,	fat,—	me,	met,—	pine,	pin,—	no,	move

2	2	2	2	3	2	3	2
shep' herd	ear' nest	hal' ter	au' tumn
south ern	seam stress	broad ness	pau per
threat en	young ish	sau çer	sau çy
daunt ed	chris ten	cau cus	talk ing
vul pine	cur tain	talk er	walk ing
heart less	heark en	yawn ing	naugh ty
wrap per	wealth y	law yer	law less
wick ed	writ ten	aus tral	cau tious

2	1	2	1	33	2	32	2
el bow	mead ow	trow el	oil y
mel low	milk pail	trow şerş	noişe less
up roar	in sight	bow elş	point ed
cart load	char coal	count er	poi şon
nar row	har row	count less	oint ment
fur low	guin ea	sound ing	joint ed
sin ew	earth quake	prow ess	noi some
fel low	win now	bow ing	oys ter
bel low	yel low	out let	joy ous

John lost his ball.   It was a fair day.
His bat went next.   Ann went for a walk.
No balls nor bats.   She lost her comb.
John is now sad.   What did she find?
How can he play?   A bat and a ball.
Take a new game.   John found a comb.
Cry not for this.   Each one is glad.
You may find it.   It all ends well.

3   4   1   2   3   32   33
nor, good,—tube, tub, bull,—oil, pound,—thin, THIS

SECTION XII.

Words of two syllables accented on the second.

4 1	4 1	4 1	4 1
ap pear'	a vail'	a wait'	a wry'
ar raign	ma lign	a wry	ma lign
con ceit	as sail	a byss	ar rear
ac quaint	blas pheme	pa trol	a vail
as say	ac quire	ap praise	re store
trans fuse	trans late	tran scribe	ca reer

1 1	1 1	1 1	1 1
de light	por tray	re peat	de feat
re lease	re course	re treat	re tain
re prieve	re trieve	re gain	re main
re view	re strain	be reave	be moan
co logne	re lief	de tail	de tain
be low	re tail	re straint	be neath
be siege	de spite	fore know	re peal
be speak	de çease	be smear	be lief
de crease	de feat	be queath	re prieve
re trieve	be moan	be stow	be low
re proach	im pugn	sha green	re course

Sit in your place.
Play in due time.
Now for the book.
We have the page.
Read in your turn.
He has gone out.

James had a kite.
I saw him with it.
The line was long.
It went high up.
Charles had a dog.
The dog ran mad.

1	2	3	4	1	2	1	2	1	2

fate, far, fall, fat,—me, met,—pine, pin,—no, move

3	1	4	2	2	1	2	1
ob scene'		lam poon'		en force'		per ceive'	
con crete		pla toon		im pugn		im peach	
con tain		at tempt		un due		in crease	
con ceit		ap prove		pur sue		in dict	
com plain		ca noe		il lume		en croach	
block ade		ca tarrh		im pair		en gross	
op pugn		bal loon		ex plain		en tail	
con geal		al lege		up braid		ex cite	
con sign		ca ress		en dear		pur suit	

2	2	2	2	4	3	2	3
im merse		your self		ba shaw		en dorse	
har poon		in stead		ab solve		en thral	
a back		a baft		as sort		un taught	
ca bal		un couth		a ward		ex hort	
im mense		in tense		ab hor		ex haust	
in verse		per verse		con form		un born	
with in		in duct		ap pall		un horse	
sur tout		fes toon		ab sorb		es cort	

The sun is up.
Let me sit in the sun.
The air is cold.
You must not go out.
Do not sit on the step.
It is too wet.
The dew is on the step.
It has wet my hat.

The top will get wet.
I will not spin it.
Let it be.
This is his cup.
It is new.
Do not spoil it.
Go and get my box.
I want my red top.

3	4	1	2	3	32	33

nor, good,—tube, tub, bull,—oil, pound,—thin, THIS

2 33	1 33	4 32	4 33
ex pound'	be foul'	a noint'	as tound'
dis count	re șound	a droit	a loud
with out	re bound	ap point	ca roușe
a bout	de nounçe	an noy	a bound
un sound	de vout	ad join	ac count
sur mount	pro found	as soil	a roușe
dis mount	re nown	al loy	a round
mis count	pro pound	ac coil	a vow
al low	re doubt	a void	a ground

4 4	1	2	1
ab stract	pro rogue	ar rest	be moan
a ghast	re main	ca reer	dis own
a baft	be hoove	ap pear	un sold
ad vançe	be caușe	im pede	in hume
har angue	re dound	im pugn	ex cișe
trans act	de șign	be lief	be stow
a back	be nign	at tempt	un bolt
cra vat	re șign	ad vançe	a new

Yes! we all love birds.

They hop, and fly, and sing.

When it is dark the birds sit in the trees.

But when the sun is up, they all fly off, and hunt for seeds, and bugs and flies.

They eat flies.

Can you fly?

No. I have no wings.

1	2	3	4	1	2	1	2	1	2
fate,	far,	fall,	fat,—	me,	met,—	pine,	pin,—	no,	move

SECTION XIII.

Words of three syllables, accented on the first.

4 1 1	4 2 1	4 2 1
an' te lope	cal' i co	nav' i gate
ab so lute	ap ti tude	an i mate
ad e quate	mag ni fy	ab di cate
cal cu late	grat i tude	al ti tude
grad u ate	man i fold	am pli fy
am pu tate	mag is trate	an te type

4 2 1	2 2 2	2 2 2
as pi rate	ĝen er ous	sud den ly
can di date	gen i tive	ter ri ble
ag gre gate	gun ne ry	trag e dy
las si tude	per ma nent	trans i tive
car a way	preṣ i dent	ver i ty
clar i fy	pun ĝen çy	lit ur ĝy
an a lyṣe	reĝ is ter	des ti ny
av er aĝe	res ti ness	in fi del
lat in ize	sed i ment	ĝen u ine

I have arms and hands.
Birds have legs and feet, but no arms.
Boys run, and birds fly.
Do you see my dog?
He is a pet dog.
We must not anger him.
He can bark, and bite.
He does not bite those who treat him well.

3	4	1	2	3	32	33	

nor, good,—tube, tub, bull,—oil, pound,—thin, THIS

2 2 2	2 2 2	2 2 2
ed' i fiçe	pes' ti lent	par' ti cle
div i dend	en er ǧy	in tel lect
en ti ty	dim i ty	dul çi mer
in ter im	ev er y	fer vent ly
lib er tine	pen i tent	lit ur ǧy
mil li ner	per ti nent	liv er y
sen ti nel	sub si dy	per fi dy
mur der ing	ef fi ǧy	set tle ment
pub lish er	ter ri ble	lev i ty

2 2 2	2 2 2	1 2 2
min is try	dis çi pline	ju ni per
fin ish er	dil i ǧent	nu di ty
clem en çy	in fi nite	u ni ty
per fect ly	pit i less	nu tri tive
ǧin ǧer ly	sim i lar	mu ti ny
vin e gar	pick er el	flu en çy
bit ter ly	slip pe ry	pu ri ty
typ i cal	pret ti ly	nu tri ment

The fox lives on the hill.

Get the dog, and let us go and hunt him.

If the dog sees him he will try to catch him.

Poor fox! the dog will hurt him.

We will kill the fox, for he comes at night, and eats the hens

See! the dog has got him!

Now fox, you will kill no more hens.

1	2	3	4	1	2	1	2	1	2

fate, far, fall, fat,—me, met,—pine, pin,—no, move

1 2 2
ho' li ness
pu er ile
cu ti cle
pi e ty
sa pi ent
se ri ous
pre mi um
hu mor ous
spu ri ous

1 2 2
po' et ess
o pi um
lone li ness
si lent ly
po per y
pu ri ty
cu ri ous
fu ri ous
o ver plus

1 2 2
use' ful ness
so ber ness
pi ous ly
ra pi er
fa vor ite
glo ri ous
du ti ful
va ri ous
ra di us

4 4 2
cav al ry
mal a dy
sal a ry
man a cle
trac ta ble
das tard ly
stag nan çy
fal la çy

4 2 2
grav i ty
van i ty
rap id ly
fac ul ty
or i gin
am i ty
chas ti ty
gal le ry

4 2 2
lav en der
man i fest
pas sen ger
man ner ly
rap id ly
mar in er
cab in et
tap es try

The day is hot.
Let me have a fan.
Jane has a fan, too.
We will blow, with our fans, and make a wind to cool us.
Ann has a fine cat.
She lives in the barn.

3　　4　　1　　2　　3　　32　　33
nor, good,—tube, tub, bull,—oil, pound,—thin, THIS

2　1　1　　　　2　1　1　　　　2　1　1
des' o late　　　der' o gate　　　reş' o lute
in vo cate　　　em u late　　　im pre cate
sep a rate　　　dis so lute　　　sur ro gate
in no vate　　　cor o nate　　　tel e scope
in du rate　　　lin e age　　　rev e nue
rep ro bate　　stip u late　　reg u late
har mon ize　　des pe rate　　dis lo cate
mem or ize　　hel le bore　　ex pe dite

1　21　　　　　3　2　2　　　　3　22
va ri ate　　　al der man　　　au di ençe
ju bi lee　　　al ma nac　　　plau si ble
pu ri fy　　　cau tious ly　　gau di ness
de i fy　　　fal si ty　　　quar ter ly
du pli cate　　straw ber ry　　hal ter ing
lu bri cate　　wa ter man　　laud a ble
de vi ate　　　nau ti cal　　　quar ter age
me di ate　　　au di tor　　　nau şeous ly

He did not see us.　　　Now we step off.
We must set out.　　　See the new barn.
Our walk is long.　　　The hay is in it.
Go on this side.　　　That cow is red.
This is the way.　　　Cows eat the hay.
No one must stop.　　A pig eats corn.
Few find the path.　　The pigs are fat.
That is the gate.　　　We must go home.
Now we will look.　　It will be dark.

| 1 | 2 | 3 | 4 | 1 | 2 | 1 | 2 | 1 | 2 |

fate, far, fall, fat,—me, met,—pine, pin,—no, move

4 2 2	4 2 4	2 1 2
nar' ra tive	rad' ic al	eb' o ny
cav i ty	stam in a	im pe tus
can is ter	an i mal	in ju ry
tan ģi ble	ad a mant	fac to ry
tran quil ly	cap i tal	ben e fit
van i ty	prac ti cal	el e gant
bar ris ter	an a gram	lep ro sy
par lia ment	cal a bash	neg a tive

2 1 2	2 1 2	2 1 2
pen u ry	pil lo ry	in te ģer
gen e sis	in so lent	im po tent
in do lent	im pu dent	sin gu lar
riv u let	his to ry	lig ne ous
mer cu ry	ten e ment	meth o dist
mem o ry	her e sy	red o lent
rec to ry	cur so ry	sub se quent
tes ta ment	lar çe ny	stren u ous

Jane has six hens.

They all lay eggs.

She put them in a pen and feeds them with corn.

The hens have nests in which they lay their eggs.

Do you like eggs?

Yes. Let us boil six eggs.

Do not boil them long or they will be hard.

3   4   1   2   3   32   33
nor, good,—tube, tub, bull,—oil, pound,—thin, THIS

2 2 1	2 2 1	2 2 1
in' sti tute	sol' i tude	es' ti mate
rid i cule	sub sti tute	med i tate
in di cate	tem per ate	rec ti tude
ser vi tude	ped i gree	ven ti late
tur pen tine	lit i gate	dis si pate
ven er ate	in di go	im i tate
vin di cate	pet ri fy	in ti mate
vit ri fy	des ti tute	cul ti vate
plen i tude	ded i cate	tur pen tine

2 2 1	2 4 2	2 4 2
ul ti mate	in fa my	tyr an ny
heṣ i tate	in fant ry	vil lain y
rev e nue	lit a ny	big a my
ir ir tate	her ald ry	firm a ment
pil grim age	in fan çy	em bas sy
curv a ture	per ma nent	sect a ry
ep i cure	sub stan tive	cul pa ble
fer til ize	sym pa thy	lux a tive

Did you ever see a fish?

They have fins and scales.

If a fish had no fins it could not swim.

They are very good to eat.

If you can get a hook and line, we will go and catch a fish in the creek.

You must first put a fly on your hook, else the fish will not bite it.

1	2	3	4	1	2	1	2	1	2
fate, far, fall, fat,—me, met,—pine, pin,—no, move

2 4 2	2 2 4	2 2 4
pen' al ty	ep' i gram	sim' i lar
fil a ment	mil i tant	lib er al
flip pan çy	fin ic al	fish er man
flip pant ly	car di nal	lit er al
frus tra tive	pel i can	pub lic an
in fan çy	fed er al	sup pli ant
in ward ly	min er al	ut ter ançe
hep tar chy	prin çi pal	el e phant

2 2 4	1 1 2	1 1 4
ĝen er al	vi o let	cu po la
ped es tạl	vi o lent	mu tu al
phyş ic al	a the işm	tu te lar
viġ il ant	bi na ry	me di al
fur ther ançe	a the ist	re şe ate
chem ic al	cu ra tive	main te nançe
myr i ad	do na tive	di a phragm
mys tic al	po e sy	fu ner al

The fish takes the fly into his mouth to eat it,
and the hook sticks fast, and we then pull him
out.

Put some coal in the stove, and let us have a
fire.

This is a cold day. We must not go out.

Some poor boys have no fire to sit by, and no
coat or shoes to put on, to keep them warm.

| 3 | 4 | 1 | 2 | 3 | 32 | 33 |

nor, good,—tube, tub, bull,—oil, pound,—thin, THIS

2 2	2 2	1 2
em' pe ror	rust' ic al	beau' ti ful
min is ter	vul gar ly	bind er y
mit ti mus	her e tic	boat a ble
tem per ançe	crit ic al	di a logue
ten der ly	clin ic al	du bi ous
lex i con	ed i tor	east er ly
hep ta gon	ef fi ġy	cu ti cle
in ter val	bit ter ness	cu ri ous

1 2	1 2	1 2
pa per mill	mu sic al	waste ful ly
ford a ble	newṣ pa per	pre vi ous
for çi ble	night in gale	rea ṣon er
griev ous ly	no ble ness	suit a ble
ju bi lee	o di ous	ti tle page
o pen ing	de vi ous	u ni corn
lu dic rous	wea ri some	u ni verse
çi pher ing	ra di ançe	ve he mençe

Poor boys! How cold they must be!

You must be kind to the poor.

God is good to us. Let us be kind to them.

God loves those who are kind to the poor.

We may be poor some day, and want help, as much a they.

James Rice is a good boy.

He is but six years old, and yet he does not lie in bed, when the sun is up.

1	2	3	4	1	2	1	2	1	2
fate,	far,	fall,	fat,—	me,	met,—	pine,	pin,—	no,	move

4 1	4 1	4 1
ad' vo cate	gal' le ry	mac' u late
bar on et	man u al	al co ran
cal o mel	san a tive	har mo ny
an nu al	grad ua l	pan o ply
ab so lute	grad u ate	strat a gem
ap pe tite	ad e quate	gland u lous
ap po şite	am pu tate	daf fo dil
fac to ry	al co hol	an o dyne

4 2 1	4	4
ram i fy	rad i cal	rap id ly
nav i gate	ra tion al	mag net işm
cal i co	tam a rind	cal um ny
sal i vate	das tard ly	cat a ract
lat i tude	par al lel	pas sen ger
man i fold	av a riçe	cav i ty
an ec dote	far ri er	ad jec tive
palp i tate	can ni bal	hap pi ness

He steps out of bed and puts on his pants and coat, and goes downstairs.

He is soon ready to go to school.

The boys all love James. He is kind to them. If he has nuts or cake, he gives them a share.

When the air is warm at night, the bugs buzz round the lamps.

| 3 | 4 | 1 | 2 | 3 | 32 | 33 |

nor, good,—tube, tub, bull,—oil, pound,—thin, THIS

2 1	2 1	2 1
ben′ e fit	rec′ to ry	vic′ to ry
des o late	reg u lar	min u end
del e gate	dis so lute	tur bu lent
el e gant	im ple ment	vit re ous
el e ment	in no çent	vas cu lar
ex pe dite	sin gu lar	sub se quent
arm o ry	vin e gar	taf fe ta
pen du lum	in do lent	neb u lous
neg a tive	im po tent	im mo late

2 1	2 1	2 1
im pu dent	lig a ture	flat u lent
pil lo ry	pen e trate	friv o lous
in cu bus	pen te cost	es cu lent
in do lençe	min u et	em u lous
lep ro sy	par o dy	el o gy
pop u late	mis cre ant	dep re cate
man a ger	in no vate	dec o rate
lux u ry	el o quent	dec o rous

If they come too close, they will burn their wings.

The bats fly in the air to find flies and bugs which they eat.

The bat looks like a mouse.

The bat has wings, but mice have none.

The wing of the bat is not like the wing of a bird. It is made of soft skin.

1	2	3	4	1	2	1	2	1	2
fate,	far,	fall,	fat,—	me,	met,—	pine,	pin,—	no,	move

2

pil' grim age
ġen tle man
pun ġen çy
in su lar
num ber less
rest less ness
rev er end
rit u al
met a phor

2

pes' ti lençe
lat er al
pin na cle
bar ber ry
but ter fly
buf fa lo
del a gate
cler ic al
an te type

2

ful' mi nate
fur bish er
mus cu lar
lac te al
rug ged ness
al i quot
med i çine
en vi ous
stim u late

2

in te ġer
op e rate
rel e vant
lit i gate
pen ni less
lit a ny
cler ġy man
dep u tize

2

crit i çism
wit ti çişm
lit i gant
hyp o crite
vir u lent
quer u lous
stren u ous
neb u lous

2

sym me try
viv i fy
vil i fy
grat i fy
pet ro nel
stul ti fy
len i ty
den si ty

Here is a fine horse which has come out to eat grass.

See how hi*gh* he holds his head.

How can we catch the horse when we want to ride him?

If we run up, and try to catch him he will trot off to the end of the field, and be out of our reach.

3	4	1	2	3	32	33

nor, good,—tube, tub, bull,—oil, pound,—thin, THIS

1 4	1 2	1 2
re′ gal ly	du′ el ing	du′ bi ous
va gran çy	nu mer al	cru çi fix
lu cra tive	ru in ous	u ni corn
fru gal ly	nu mer ous	ru di ment
pri ma ry	dan ger ous	state li ness
di al ist	ve hi cle	cu bic al
no ta ble	cu ti cle	pe ri od
pli a ble	de i fy	ra di ançe
pa gan ism	ju bi lee	lone li ness

1	1	1
se cre çy	ri ot ous	cu po la
pi ous ly	no ble man	su per fine
mi cro scope	so ber ly	spu ri ous
mu çil age	roşe ma ry	cu ti cle
su i çide	di a per	ro şe ate
tu te lar	low er most	night in gale
bo re as	dra per y	tu ber ous
me te or	pa per mill	mu ti late
sa pi ent	lo cal ly	u ni form

Horses eat hay, oats, corn, and grass, and are of a great help to us, in doing our work.

George Lane has just come home from school. His eye is bright with joy, and a smile plays on his lips.

| 1 | 2 | 3 | 4 | 1 | 2 | 1 | 2 | 1 | 2 |
fate, far, fall, fat,—me, met,—pine, pin,—no, move

SECTION XIV.

Words of three syllables accented on the second.

1 1 4	1 1 4	1 1 4
pro po' sal	o me' ga	re fu' tal
de cri al	de ni al	sa li va
re pri şal	di plo ma	co e qual
co e val	hy e na	re li ançe
de cre tal	i de al	pe ru şal

4 2 2	4 2 2	4 2 2
an ǥel ic	a part ment	ap pen dix
mag net ic	ca thar tic	as sem bly
af flict ed	af fect ed	ma li çious
at ten tive	a ven ger	ban dit ti
fa nat ic	sa tir ic	a sun der
a mend ment	ant arc tic	at tem per
ad mis sion	ad di tion	am bi tion
am bi tious	par ti tion	tra di tion

Would you like to know why he is so pleased?

He had studied very hard for a long time, and now has just gained the prize for his industry and good conduct.

Everyone loves George; for he is kind, as well as studious.

Will you not try and be such a boy as George Lane?

3	4	1	2	3	32	33

nor, good,—tube, tub, bull,—oil, pound,—thin, THIS

2 2 2	2 2 2	2 2 2
in trep' id	im pul' sive	em bel' lish
in trin şic	im pli çit	ex ten sive
im per fect	im bit ter	a ven ger
dis pir it	ex pli çit	en kin dle
di min ish	dis şem ble	im bit ter
dis tem per	dis tin guish	ef fect ive
ec çen tric	em bez zle	dis tinc tive
dis burse ment	ex pen sive	im pul sive
en cum bent	ex pres sive	in flict er

2 2 2	2 2 2	1 2
in tent ly	in dul gent	re duc tion
in sert ed	in jus tiçe	re flec tion
in cum ber	in ter ment	e duc tion
in duc tive	in trin şic	e rup tion
en gen der	dis cred it	e lec tion
in sip id	dis cus ser	pre dic tion
in vest ment	dis sent er	re jec tion
en dem ic	dis til ler	se lec tion

A merry May Day to you all!

The birds all seem to sing a welcome to the sweet month of May.

The little lambs, with their soft white wool, skip and play over the green grass, as if they too, knew this was May Day.

The cold March winds are gone, and birds, trees, flowers, lambs, and little boys all rejoice.

1	2	3	4	1	2	1	2	1	2

fate, far, fall, fat,—me, met,—pine, pin,—no, move

1	2	2	1	2	2	1	2	2

re plen' ish	e met' ic	de cant' er
de mer it	po et ic	de çep tive
spe çif ic	de fend er	be gin ning
de liv er	de crep it	de fect ive
fo ren şic	re new er	de fen sive
pro hib it	re plev in	de scrip tive
re mit tançe	e clip tic	fre quent er
e lec tric	e lix ir	i tal ic
e mul ǥent	be gin ner	pe dant ic

1	2	2	1	2	2	1	2	2

pre tend er	sa tan ic	re spect er
pre şerv er	pro tract er	re vul sive
pre ven tive	re mit ter	ro man tic
pro hib it	re dun dant	so li çit
pro ject ile	pro tract ive	tri umph ant
pro lif ic	re mit ted	u şurp er
pro phet ic	re lin quish	su per nal

How bright the sun seems, as it rises over the hills.

The dewdrops glitter in its rays as they lie on the blades of grass.

The air is pure and mild and sweet flowers are seen in every field.

Who does not love the pretty flowers?

We must thank God for sparing our lives to see this happy day.

3	4	1	2	3	32	33		

nor, good,—tube, tub, bull,—oil, pound,—thin, THIS

1 1 2	1 1 2	1 1 2
de co′ rum	o bli′ ging	co he′ şive
mu şe um	de po nent	re fi ner
de lu der	se du çer	be la ted
re la ter	pro fa ner	ca na ry
pro du çer	de ri der	de façe ment
po ma tum	pro vi der	de fa mer
re lu çent	re sto rer	de fi ler
su pine ly	se date ly	co he rent

4 2	1 1	1 1
ab strac tion	pro ba tion	vi bra tion
ab rup tion	pri va tion	e mo tion
at ten tion	ro ta tion	se cre tion
af flic tion	cre a tion	çi ta tion
at trac tive	de vo tion	lo ca tion
as ser tion	pro mo tion	ne ga tion
par ti tion	le ga tion	no ta tion

Those that grow in the garden do not seem half so fair as the sweet field flowers.

Do you see the sun?

How large and bright it is!

Yes, and it is warm too.

If we had no sun we would have no day.

It would be dark night.

If the rays of the sun were not warm the grass would not grow, and we would all die of cold.

1	2	3	4	1	2	1	2	1	2

fate, far, fall, fat,—me, met,—pine, pin,—no, move

1 2	1 1	4 1 2
pro tec' tion	sa ga' çious	ad he' rent
re ten tion	fe ro çious	mand a mus
re gres sion	vo ra çious	ap pa rent
se lec tion	lo qua çious	a ba sive
re demp tion	ca pa çious	al lu rer
tri sec tion	te na çious	a maze ment
pro lif ic	vi va çious	a tone ment
re flec tion	fa çe tious	ad ja çent

4 1 2	4 4 2	2 1 2
a dor er	a mass ment	en fee ble
nar ra tor	a larm ing	bit u men
a cu men	At lan tic	tes ta trix
ac qui rer	ap par el	in vi ter
fal la çious	as sas sin	pur su er
a bate ment	at tract ed	sur vi vor
a gree ment	trans plant ed	un du ly
ar ranç ing	at tract ive	un ho ly

If the sun was near us we would burn up with its heat.

The mole lives in the ground.

He looks like a rat, but he has a shorter tail.

His eyes are very small, and his long fur keeps the dirt out of them.

Here is a mole.

3	4	1	2	3	32	33

nor, good,—tube, tub, bull,—oil, pound,—thin, THIS

2 1 2	1 3 2	2 4 2
en li' ven	de mol' ish	in hab' it
en a ble	re spons ive	en camp ment
re la ted	de poşit	in graft ed
trans la ted	re call ing	in val id
in fla ted	be fall en	ex act ness
in he rent	re şolv ing	in ac tive
il lu mine	e norm ous	em pan nel
il lu sive	re cord er	im aġ ine

2 4 2	2 3 2	1 2 4
gri mal kin	in doç ile	e ter nal
en chant ment	nar cot ic	pa rent al
un mask ing	syn op sis	re luct ant
ec stat ic	dis hon est	e nig ma
en am el	diş şolv ent	re pug nant
en tan gle	har mon ic	re new al
ex am ple	im mod est	di ur nal

See how he digs up the grass, and hides himself.

Now he is quite gone.

He dug the hole with his nose and his paws.

I have just bought a box of figs.

Come and get some.

Are you fond of figs?

Yes sir, I like them very much.

You have seen grapes.

1	2	3	4	1	2	1	2	1	2
fate,	far,	fall,	fat,—	me,	met,—	pine,	pin,—	no,	move

2 2 4	4 2 4	4 2 4
ex ter′ nal	pa ter′ nal	ad mit′ tançe
in fer nal	a bund ançe	at tend ant
in tend ant	fra ter nal	as çend ant
ap pend ant	at tend ançe	ab er rant
dis turb ançe	af firm ant	as sist ançe
in çes sant	as sist ant	ma ter nal
ap pel pant	ma lig nant	at tend ançe
in dig nant	ac quit tal	ac çept ançe

4 2 2	3 1	4 1
ath let ic	col la tion	sal va tion
pa çif ic	com mo tion	stag na tion
pa thet ic	com ple tion	tax a tion
a mend er	con cre tion	trans la tion
a sun der	col lu şion	gra da tion
ma jes tic	con tu şion	car na tion
trans mit ted	con clu sion	ab lu tion
as trin ģent	con fu şion	plant a tion

Figs are a fruit like large grapes put up on sugar.

They are sweet and good.

Take some more in your hand and I will put away the box.

You may take some home to James.

Here is a rose on the bush.

It has just come out.

You may pull the rose and smell it.

THE OWL.

I have been in the barn. There I saw an owl. John says, it sits all day on the beam. You would laugh to see it wink. It has great big eyes and yet it seems as if it could not see, though it is daylight and the sun shines.

Its eyes are made to see best in the dark, like those of a cat. Bats and owls catch their prey by night. The barn owl eats the rats and mice, and so saves the wheat, oats and corn. Some owls live in holes in old trees.

Brown owls live all day in the woods, but at night they come near the house and make a great noise. Sometimes they do harm.

Last night an owl got into the dove house, and took three doves.

1	2	3	4	1	2	1	2	1	2

fate, far, fall, fat,—me, met,—pine, pin,—no, move

The vowel in the third syllable, when not silent has the sound of short u.

2 2	1 1	1 2
en vel' op	cre a' tor	de vel' op
in spect or	e qua tor	pro fess or
di rect or	di la tor	pro tect or
en deav or	ro ta tor	pre cept or
suc çess or	de çi pher	co part ner

2 1	3 2	2 2
en vi ron	ob ject or	en ģen der
dic ta tor	tor ment or	en cum ber
spec ta tor	con duct or	dis tem per
tes ta tor	col lect or	dis cus ser
en dan ģer	con sid er	dis pen ser
di vi şor	op press or	dis turb er

See, you have let it fall, and there is dirt on the face of it.

Shake the mud off, and keep it clean.

May I have a pink, too?

Yes, and here is one for John.

Thank you sir, you are very kind.

Sir, will you please let me use a pen?

I wish to write.

Can you write your name?

Yes sir.

Put the pen in the ink stand, and get some ink.

Now let me see you try.

3	4	1	2	3	32	33

nor, good,—tube, tub, bull,—oil, pound,—thin, THIS

3 1
Oc to' ber
ho ri zon
col la tor
con troll er

3 2
pos sess or
of fend er
con fess or
cor rect or

2 1
dis po şer
em bla zon

2 1
di vi şor
sur vi vor

2 1
ex cu şer
ex port er

1 2
re mem' ber
pre cur sor
be wil der
No vem ber

1 2
pre çent or
re flect or
e lect or
pre dict or

4 4 3
at tract or
a ban don

4
trans gress or
ag gress or

4
nar ra tor
ac cus tom

2 2
in vent' or
dis rup tion
ar rest ed
sur ren der

2 2
en ven om
mis reck on
dis sent er
sus pend ers

1 3 2
re cord er
re tort er

1 4
pro tract or
ro man çer

2 3 2
en joy er
em ploy er

You do not hold the pen right.

You must write with great care if you wish to learn.

Now go and get your slate and I will teach you how to do arithmetic.

James and George have a boat in the pond.
They can both row very well.
It is fine sport to sail about and take the air.

1	2	3	4	1	2	1	2	1	2

fate, far, fall, fat,—me, met,—pine, pin,—no, move

SECTION XV.

Words of three syllables accented on the third.

2 1 2	2 2 1	2 2 1
rep re hend'	in ter vene'	dis in cline'
in di rect	in ter fere	ev er more
rep re şent	in ter poşe	en ter tain
man u mit	in dis creet	in dis poşe
ap pre hend	dis en gage	bar ri cade
dis re spect	in ter line	ap per tain
dis re gard	ref er ee	in sin çere
con tra dict	fric as see	un der take

2 1 1	2 1 1	2 2 1
dev o tee	in se cure	dis a gree
ser e nade	dis be lief	in ter çede
dis re pute	an te çede	rep ar tee
dis o blige	per se vere	mis ap ply
dis u nite	im po lite	un der go
im ma ture	deb o nair	brig a dier
in tro duçe	ref u gee	dis a buşe
mis be have	dis be lieve	gren a dier

One day James let his hat fall in the pond.
His dog Trip soon got it for him.
Trip is a good dog and swims well.
He loves James. His dog will bite no one.

The sheep live on grass.
They yield us warm wool to make coats to keep
out the cold.

3   4   1   2   3   32   33
nor, good,—tube, tub, bull,—oil, pound,—thin, THIS

SECTION XVI.

Words of four syllables accented on the first.

4   2   4   2
ad' ver sa ry

com mis sa ry

an ti qua ry

ad mi ra ble

ac çes so ry

4   2   4   2
ar' bi tra ry

cap il la ry

an swer a bly

ad mi ral ty

cap i tal ly

4   2   4   2
nav i ga ble

prac ti ca ble

hab it a ble

lap id a ry

ac cu ra çy

mar ket a ble

am i ca ble

2   2   2   2
ep i lep sy

in ter est ing

rev er ent ly

pen i tent ly

em i nent ly

im pi ous ly

in çi den çy

A lamb is a young sheep.

Lambs are white and clean.

The lamb will eat salt or meal out of your hand, if you are kind to it.

But if you are not kind, it will run as soon as it sees you.

The lambs skip and play and so do boys and girls.

Play is good for them, but they must take care not to play too much.

1	2	3	4	1	2	1	2	1	2
fate,	far,	fall,	fat,—	me,	met,—	pine,	pin,—	no,	move

2	2	2	2
dif'	fer	ent	ly
dil	i	ģent	ly
par	ti	ci	ple
ex	çel	len	çy
el	i	ģi	bly
ģen	er	ous	ly
en	vi	ous	ly
in	fin	it*e*	ly

2	2	2	2
ex'	çel	lent	ly
preş	by	ter	y
sens	i	ble	ness
mis	e	ra	bly
el	i	ģi	ble
em	i	nent	ly
ex	quiş	it*e*	ly
neg	li	ģent	ly

2	2	4	2
ef	fi	ca	çy
cred	it	a	ble
des	pi	ca	ple
ģen	er	al	ly
lit	er	al	ly
miş	er	a	ble
in	ti	ma	çy
in	tri	ca	çy

2	2	4	2
mil	i	ta	ry
mer	çe	na	ry
com	pa	ra	ble
cen	sur	a	ble
ģen	tl*e*	man	ly
mil	le	na	ry
ex	e	cra	bl*e*
mis	çel	la	ny

See how fat the old hog is!

He can just get up in his sty because he is so big and fat.

He can lie down, and he can eat as he lies.

Now he is done and he will go to sleep.

Oh lazy old hog!

Do not lie, and eat and sleep so, all day.

3   4   1   2   3   32 33

nor, good,—tube, tub, bull,—oil, pound,—thin, THIS

2 2 4 2	2 2 4 2
leg' end a ry	vig' il ant ly
ex em pla ry	im pli ca ted
ex pli ca tive	ven e ra ble
des pi ca ble	miş er a bly
cred it a ble	mys tic al ly
in tri ca çy	per ish a ble
ir ri ta ble	pit i a ble
ex pi a ble	preb en da ry

2 2 4 2	1 2 4 2
ven er a ble	lu min a ry
sem i na ry	mo ment a ry
pref er a ble	a vi a ry
sed en ta ry	a mi a ble
ser viçe a ble	fa vor a ble
vul ner a ble	va ri a ble
veġ e ta ble	mu şic al ly
ut ter a ble	nu mer a ble

The poor bird has lost her nest.

Some boy saw it on the bush and took it, and all the eggs that she had in it.

He did not want the nest, but he took it to play with the eggs.

Do you see how sad the poor bird is. Do you not hear her cry?

Poor bird! I wish the boy had not seen your nest.

1	2	3	4	1	2	1	2	1	2

fate, far, fall, fat,—me, met,—pine, pin,—no, move

3   2 2 2

con' fi dent ly

com pe ten çy

con se quent ly

ob vi ous ly

com pe tent ly

pros per ous ly

pon der ous ly

4   2 4 2

an' cil la ry

ad mi ra ble

am i ca ble

am i ca bly

ap pli ca ble

char i ta bly

hab er dash er

4   2

ap o plex y

an i ma ted

an ti mo ny

cap i tal ly

am or ous ly

ad e quate ly

man da to ry

nat u ral ly

4   2

mat ri mo ny

mal le a ble

Jan u a ry

ac cu rate ly

jan i za ry

slan der ous ly

lam ent a ble

nav i ga ble

What a fine large cat is here.

Touch her; how sleek she is!

What soft fur she has!

Take care she has sharp claws.

If you are kind to her, she will not hurt you.

Tell Jane to bring her some milk.

She drinks milk when she can get it.

Do not feed the cat too much or she will not catch any mice.

3   4   1   2   3   32 33
nor, good,—tube, tub, bull,—oil, pound,—thin, THIS

2   1
çer' e mo ny
ig no min y
fig u ra tive
in no çent ly
mem o ra ble
pit e ous ly
rev o ca ble
spec u la tive

2   1
im po tent ly
reg u la tor
ģen u ine ly
veģ e ta tive
im po ten çy
ex cre to ry
sec u lar ly
sin gu lar ly

2   1
es' tu a ry
sec re ta ry
tem po ra ry
tit u la ry
trib u ta ry
un du la ry
nec ro man çer
fec u len çy

2   1
per se cu tor
des o late ly
reg u la tor
ex e cra ted
ren o va ted
sit u a ted
sed u lous ly
car i ca ture

Here comes the dog.

He barks, but he will not hurt you.

See! He wags his tail and licks your hand when you pat him on the head.

He likes to go out with us by day and he guards the house by night.

He must not come in the house. Dogs should stay out.

1	2	3	4	1	2	1	2	1	2
fate,	far,	fall,	fat,—	me,	met,—	pine,	pin,—	no,	move

3

oc' cu pan çy
nom i na tive
cop u la tive
joc u lar ly
nom in al ly
ob du ra çy
op er a tive
ob sti na çy

3

prof' it a ble
prod i gal ly
tol er a ble
com men ta ry
com mis sa ry
sol i ta ry
mon i to ry
prom is so ry

3

prom on to ry
or tho dox y
cor o na ry
hon or a ry
hos pit a ble
com mon al ty
cor ri ġi ble

3

prov i dent ly
mon as te ry
or a to ry
form u la ry
pop u lous ness
ob vi ous ness
poş i tive ly

How hot it is today!

The sun is so warm that it makes my head ache. I take off my hat. It is so hot that I cannot bear to have it on.

What shall I do?

I cannot drive my hoop; nor work in my garden. I cannot play at bat and ball. There is no wind to fly my kite.

You may lie down in the shade by the side of the pond and read.

It is never too warm to read.

3	4	1	2	3	32	33

nor, good,—tube, tub, bull,—oil, pound,—thin, THIS

SECTION XVII.

Words of four syllables accented on the second.

2	4	2	2

in tran' și tive

bar bar i ty

men daç i ty

dis par i ty

dis sat is fy

2	4	2	2

hi lar' i ty

vi vaç i ty

hex am e ter

in fal li bly

vul gar i ty

1	4	2	1

e man çi pate

pro cras ti nate

be at i tude

de cap i tate

e rad i cate

pre var i cate

e mas cu late

re an i mate

1	2	2	1

de crep i tude

de gen er ate

de bil i tate

re verb er ate

pre çip i tate

pre med i tate

re crim in ate

re it er ate

William Stone had a fine kite.

On a clear bright day in the fall of the year, when the wind blew, he went out to fly it.

His brother James wished to go along to help him.

But William said, "No, I can fly it my-self.

1	2	3	4	1	2	1	2	1	2

fate, far, fall, fat,—me, met,—pine, pin,—no, move

1 2 2 2
mu nif' i çent
so lem ni ty
re çip i ent
pro lix i ty
pro fund i ty
se ren i ty
pro pens i ty
pro fess ed ly

1 2 2 2
so lid' i ty
sta bil i ty
stu pid i ty
te mer i ty
re vers i ble
de fin i tive
de cliv i ty
cu pid i ty

1 2 2 2
de pend en çy
ma lig ni ty
lu çid i ty
fu til i ty
de lir i ous
çe ler i ty
çe leb ri ty
be nef i çent

1 2 2 2
bi en ni al
ca lid i ty
be nef i çençe
pre çip it ous
tri en ni al
re mem ber ing
pre sent i ment
bru tal i ty

He tried two or three times, but only dragged it on the ground and tore it.

At last when his kite was almost ruined he was forced to ask his brother to help him.

James forgave William's lack of kindness and gave him all the help he could. The kite was soon seen flying high in the air, far above the tops of the tallest trees.

3   4   1   2   3   32   33
nor, good,—tube, tub, bull,—oil, pound,—thin, THIS

1 2   2   2
re lin' quish ing
fru gal i ty
no bil i ty
de bil i ty
vo çif er ous
be nig ni ty
co in ci dent
de struc tive ly

1 2 2 2
do çil' i ty
fra ġil i ty
e ter ni ty
e phem e ris
e mer ġen çy
di viş i ble
u til i ty
sta tis tic al

4   1 2 2
va cu i ty
ma tu ri ty
anx i e ty
gra tu it ous
la bo ri ous
har mo ni ous
cal ca re ous
tranş pa ren çy

4   1   2   2
ab ste mi ous
al lu sive ly
tra ġe di an
sa lu bri ous
par tu ri ent
ap pa rent ly
la bo ri ous
ad mi ring ly

How sweet and cool the air feels on my face, as it blows from the pond.

You must not lie long here. The grass feels damp.

You might catch a cold and become very sick.

At the close of day, before you go to sleep, you should not fail to pray to God, to keep you from sin and from harm.

1	2	3	4	1	2	1	2	1	2

fate, far, fall, fat,—me, met,—pine, pin,—no, move

2 2 2 2
rus tiç' i ty
un ġen er ous
ty ran ni cal
per plex i ty
fer til i ty
ġen til i ty
ex trem i ty
ex pliç it ly

2 2 2 2
in fin i tive
in dig ni ty
in dif fer ençe
in flex i ble
in sens i ble
in teg ri ty
in tel li ġence

2   2 2 2
ex per' i ment
ex press ive ly
in def in ite
in cred i ble
im pen i tent
im ped i ment
dis till er y
dis trib u tive

2   2   2 2
per cep ti ble
re ġid i ty
scur ril i ty
ri dic u lous
per plex i ty
un çer tain ty
un çiv il ly

You ask your friends for food and drink, and when they give you what you ask for, you thank them and love them for the good they show to you.

But God is the best of all friends. Oh love him and thank Him always.

You do not read well today.

If you do not try to read, you will be a poor student, and no one will like you, or care for you.

3	4	1	2	3	32	33

nor, good,—tube, tub, bull,—oil, pound,—thin, THIS

1 1 2 2

sa ti' e ty

va ri e ty

e bri e ty

so bri e ty

pro pri e ty

no to ri ous

vice ge ren cy

vo lu min ous

1 1 2 2

pre ca' ri ous

vi ca ri ous

se cu ri ty

de mo ni ac

de du çi ble

pe nu ri ous

ne fa ri ous

te nu i ty

1 1 21

re pu di ate

vi tu per ate

re mu ner ate

de pre çi ate

e lu tri ate

e lu çi date

e ma çi ate

1 1 2 2

fa tu ri ty

gre ga ri ous

eu lo ġi um

va cu i ty

fe lo ni ous

me lo di ous

cre du li ty

Bring me your book that I may mark the place. Now go and sit down on that seat.

Do not get so near the door, or you may catch a cold.

Here are some boys who seem to hunt for something.

Have you lost anything, boys?

No sir.

But we want to find a bird's nest, to get the eggs.

1	2	3	4	1	2	1	2	1	2
fate,	far,	fall,	fat,—	me,	met,—	pine,	pin,—	no,	move

3 2 2 2

con vex' i ty
con tempt i ble
con vert i ble
com press i ble
pros per i ty
con ven ti cle
con fess ed ly
prox im i ty

3   3

com mod' i ty
con com it ant
con glom er ate
con form i ty
cor rob o rate
coş mop o lite
con sol i date
prog nos tic ate

3 2 1 2

con tig u ous
om nip o tençe
con sec u tive
om nip o tent
con spic u ous
com pul so ry
so lil o quy

3   3

dox ol o by
on tol o gy
coş mog ra phy
com poş i tor
cog noş çi ble
mor bos i ty
to pog ra phy

What! Would you take the eggs from the poor little birds?

That would be wrong.

If you find any nests, with eggs or with young birds, you may look at them, but do not take them.

God made the sun, and gave it light,
He made the moon to shine by night,
He placed the sparkling stars on high,
And leads them through the deep blue sky.

3	4	1	2	3	32	33

nor, good,—tube, tub, bull,—oil, pound,—thin, THIS

3	1	2 2

com mo' di ous
op pro bri ous
con ve ni ent
com mu ni ty
cor ro sive ly
con cu pis çençe
con gru i ty
com pla çen çy

3	1

con ceiv' a ble
ob tain a ble
con nu bi al
col le ģi al
con troll a ble
con ģeal a ble
com mu ni cant
col lo qui al

The vowel in the fourth syllable of the following words has the short sound of *u* in tub.

2	1	2

çen tu ri on
ex te ri or
in fe ri or
in te ri or

1 3	4

bi og ra pher
chi rog ra pher
ģe og ra pher
zo og ra pher

4

ad min is ter
an te ri or
con tempt u ous

2	2	2

ar tif i cer
dis sim i lar
coṣ mog ra pher

He made the earth in order stand,
He made the ocean and the land,
He made the hills their places know,
And gentle rivers round them flow.
God made all living things with care,
He feeds the birds that wing the air,

1	2	3	4	1	2	1	2	1	2

fate, far, fall, fat,—me, met,—pine, pin,—no, move

SECTION XVIII.

Words of four syllables, accented on the third.

N. B. In the last syllable of the words on this page, *tion* is pronounced *shun.*

2 2 1
per spi ra' tion
im i ta tion
div i na tion
dis pens a tion
der i va tion

2 2 1
pub lic a' tion
dis si pa tion
se ques tra tion
ex ult a tion
ter min a tion

2 2 1
dec li na tion
dim in u tion
rep li ca tion
ful mi na tion
em i gra tion
lit i ga tion
per tur ba tion
dis tri bu tion

2 2 1
in car na tion
in dig na tion
lib er a tion
in crus ta tion
in un da tion
vin di ca tion
des ti na tion
per ti na çious

He gave the beasts their dens and caves,
And fish their dwelling in the waves.
He called all beings into birth,
That crowd the ocean, air and earth,
And all his works join to proclaim,
The glory of his holy name.

3	4	1	2	3	32	33	

nor, good,—tube, tub, bull,—oil, pound,—thin, THIS

2	2	2	4

in ter stel' lar
reg i ment al
in çi dent al
det ri ment al
fun da ment al
sem pi ter nal
pen i ten tial
cir cum stan tial

2	2	2

in ter rup tion
in ter mis sion
reş ur rec tion
ben e dic tion
in ter sec tion
dif i ni tion
in di ges tion
çir cum spec tion

2	2	2	2

in ter mit tent
ep i dem ic
in ter min gle
sys tem at ic
en er get ic
in ter mit ting
in ter reg num
in di rect ly

2	2	2

ex hi bi tion
in ter çes sion
im per fec tion
in ter jec tion
mis di rec tion
in ter ven tion
sur rep ti tious
rec ol lec tion

The chill winds blow.

There is ice on the pond, and snow on the ground.

The trees are white, and the grass is hid.

Go and get your skates.

Bind them fast to your feet.

Now skim away.

The ice is smooth.

Careful or you will fall.

1	2	3	4	1	2	1	2	1	2

fate, far, fall, fat,—me, met,—pine, pin,—no, move

4   2   1

fab ri ca tion
mas ti ca tion
grav i ta tion
an i ma tion
ab er ra tion
sal i va tion
ab di ca tion
pal pi ta tion

4   2   1

nav i ga' tion
ap pel la tion
al li ga tion
hab it a tion
fas çin a tion
ap pli ca tion
ad mi ra tion
lam ent a tion

4   1   1

av o ca tion
grad u a tion
sal u ta tion
ad o ra tion
val u a tion
am bu la tion
ab so lu tion
ag gre ga tion

3   2   1

os ten ta tion
tol er a tion
con stel la tion
con vers a tion
con dem na tion
prot est a tion
con sum ma tion
con fis ca tion

Now it rains. I fear we shall have a wet day, and then we cannot go out to play at all.

What shall we do indoors all day long.

I wish it would not rain. I do not love wet days.

But yet the rain does much good.

If we had no rain, we should have no grass, and we would all die.

3	4	1	2	3	32	33

nor, good,—tube, tub, bull,—oil, pound,—thin, THIS

2	1	1

in no va' tion
rev e la tion
çel e bra tion
im pu ta tion
dis pu ta tion
del e ga tion
suf fo ca tion
sup po și tion

2	1	1

rev o lu tion
em u la tion
dep re da tion
dec o ra tion
el o cu tion
ex e cu tion
reș o lu tion
el e va tor

2	1	1

veg e ta tion
rec re a tion
des o la tion
el e va tion
im port a tion
reg u la tion
des pe ra tion
stim u la tion

2	1	1

trib u la tion
res to ra tion
im pli ca tion
per se cu tion
ex por ta tion
rep u ta tion
deg ra da tion
ed u ca tion

The rain cools the air, and we can play without getting hot.

If boys were never in the house, how would they learn anything?

But you have a warm house to go in when it rains so that you may be dry.

Now the rain is past, and all things look good once more.

1	2	3	4	1	2	1	2	1	2
fate,	far,	fall,	fat,—	me,	met,—	pine,	pin,—	no,	move

2   1   1

un pro vi' ded

mis de mean or

in co he rençe

an te çe dent

dis a gree ment

in co he rent

in de co rum

in se cure ly

2   1   1

in no va' tor

pec u la tor

per se cu tor

reg u la tor

punc tu a tion

rev o ca tion

sit u a tion

trib u la tion

  4   1   2

mal e dic tion

man u mis sion

val e dic tion

ap pa ri tion

ap pre hen sion

an te mun dane

ad o les çençe

4   1   2

ap o plec tic

pat ro nym ic

ad mo ni tion

ab o li tion

am mu ni tion

ap po și tion

ac a dem ic

God made the world in six days.

He made grass and trees, and stars, and fish, and birds and beasts.

The same God who did all these great works, loves and takes care of us all.

No one is so small that He does not see him.

No one is so strong that he does not need His help.

We must love and serve the great God Who is so kind to us.

3	4	1	2	3	32	33

nor, good,—tube, tub, bull,—oil, pound,—thin, THIS

2	2	1

il lus tra' tion
in ti ma tion
mit i ga tion
dis si pa tion
cul ti va tion
per spi ra tion
in dig na tion
div i na tion

2	2	1

ven er a tion
viṣ it a tion
pub li ca tion
res ti tu tion
sep a ra tion
sup pli ca tion
sem i co lon

2	2	1

in crus ta' tion
lit i ga tion
ex pli ca tion
dim in u tion
in sti tu tion
in vi ta tion
des ti na tion
med i ta tion

2	2	1

un di vi ded
em i gra tion
lib er a tion
in car na tion
per tur ba tion
reç it a tion
en er va tion

Here is a ripe peach for Charles.

When you have eaten it you may throw the stone out of the window.

The peach stone is the seed of the tree.

If you plant a peach stone with care, you will soon have a small peach tree, which in a few years will bear fruit.

The seed of the peach and plum is covered with a hard shell which we call the stone.

1	2	3	4	1	2	1	2	1	2

fate, far, fall, fat,—me, met,—pine, pin,—no, move

1 2   2
su per sti' tion
u ni ver sal
su per car go
re im burse ment
co a les çençe
pre di lec tion
su per ven tion
pro hi bi tion

1 2
de vi a' tion
re per cus sion
fu mi ga tion
mu ti la tion
fo ment a tion
re im pres sion
du pli ca tion
gu ber na tion

3   1 1
com pu ta tion
mod u la tion
cor o na tion
prov o ca tion
con fu ta tion
con gre ga tion
con se cra tion
pop u la tion

3   2   1
con tem pla tion
con dens a tion
ob li ga tion
con sult a tion
con ster na tion
dom i na tion
com pens a tion
con çen tra tion

See how the clouds gather in the west!

Their huge folds move slowly over the sky and soon all will be dark.

Hark! The loud voice of the thunder peals through the air.

The wind moans sadly through the trees and the big raindrops come swiftly to the earth.

3   4   1   2   3   32   33
nor, good,—tube, tub, bull,—oil, pound,—thin, THIS

SECTION XIX.

Words of four syllables, accented on the fourth.

4   2

an i mad vert'
char i ot eer
a voir du poiş
an te pe nult

2

in op por tune'
leg er de main
mis ap pre hend
nev er the less

1   2

su per in tend
su per in duçe
su per a bound

2

mis un der stand
mis com pre hend
mis rep re şent

James has just come from school where he has
been all day.

James can read quite well, and feels glad that
he has learned so much.

His friends like him and praise him because he
is a good boy.

He is always kind to his friends at school, so
that they all like him.

If he has a piece of cake, or some nuts, he does
not eat them all himself, but shares them with
all his friends.

He likes his friends for being so kind to him.

When he lies down in bed at night he asks God
to bless them; for James loves God.

THE BOY WHO STOLE THE PIN.

A bad man who was to die for his crimes, said that all his evil deeds had come from stealing a pin.

Said he, "when I was quite a small boy at school, I saw a pin in the coat-cuff of the boy who sat next to me. I did not want to ask him for it; so when no one saw me, I put out my hand and took it. But, Oh how I felt! I thought all the boys in school looked at me, as if they meant to say *'You stole a pin.'*

How glad I would have been if the pin had been back in the coat-cuff. But I was afraid the boy would see me if I tried to put it back; so I kept it. I was not found out, and soon forgot how bad I had felt. I next saw a knife and took it. I did not feel so bad, as when I stole the pin. I next stole a pair of shoes, and then a roll of cloth, and so went on from bad to worse, until I was caught and put in jail, which I do not hope to leave, until I go out to die!"

My little friend! Did you ever steal a pin? If you have not, I hope you never will. It offends God, and is the first step on the road to the jail.

3	4	1	2	3	32	33

nor, good,—tube, tub, bull,—oil, pound,—thin, THIS

SECTION XX.

Difficult and irregular monosyllables.

1	1	1	1
beard	fiend	moult	vogue
field	brief	tease	thief
court	juice	chyle	rogue
know	sign	ghost	light

2	2	2	2
psalm	jaunt	sieve	touch
soothe	noose	guest	guess
gaunt	realm	group	halve
pearl	sweat	herb	burgh
phlegm	heart	bread	cleanse
stealth	threat	hearth	dearth
meant	thread	breast	earth
breadth	tread	spread	search

If you have friends who are so kind as to take care of you, and teach you; you must thank them, as well as God for it.

You must do as they bid you as well when you are out of their sight as when they see you. You must not look cross, or cry, or fret, when they bid you do anything for they are older than you, and know best what you ought to do.

1	2	3	4	1	2	1	2	1	2
fate,	far,	fall,	fat,—	me,	met,—	pine,	pin,—	no,	move

1	1	1	1
pierçe	shriek	growth	sneeze
tierçe	lieu	quaint	league
shield	bruiṣe	height	greaṣe
clothe	priest	scroll	traipse
nieçe	thieve	throat	though
frieze	view	spright	writhe
bright	cruiṣe	sigh	nigh
loathe	sluiçe	sleight	spright

3	3	3	1
spawn	walk	sprawl	gourd
chalk	lawn	thwart	floor
wharf	aught	clauṣe	bourne
could	would	qualm	whole
sauçe	yawl	brought	roan
bawl	gauze	corpse	growth
shawl	should	ought	door
pauṣe	awl	yawn	mould

If you are cross when you are told to do anything, you will anger your kind friends, and God will not be pleased with you.

You should always try to please your friends; and as they take care of you and watch over you when you are young, you must take care of them and help them, when they grow old.

| 3 | 4 | 1 | 2 | 3 | 32 | 33 |

nor, good,—tube, tub, bull,—oil, pound,—thin, THIS

1	1	1	1
bleak	brain	fourth	scene
bleat	gauge	brogue	çeil
blithe	guişe	tight	field
çease	thigh	spright	wight
blear	blight	night	fright
boast	fierçe	grieve	might
blown	flight	soup	lease
board	slight	fruit	fleece

1	1	1	1
wield	weal	sourçe	wrote
scheme	year	smear	squeak
knight	plague	sprain	mead
isle	siege	guise	wright
staid	hoax	waif	snow
strain	folks	waive	coals
stew	speak	write	sheaf

Do you wish to see a very fine piece of work; more complete than any clock or watch?

Then look at your own hand.

How well it is suited to seize and hold anything!

You can turn it about in any direction.

There are a great number of small bones in your hand, tied together by little threads called sinews.

1	2	3	4	1	2	1	2	1	2
fate,	far,	fall,	fat,—	me,	met,—	pine,	pin,—	no,	move

2	2	2	2
flaunt	twitch	farçe	wreck
launch	hearse	guard	earn
dwarf	sketch	starve	knack
schism	through	carve	wreck
glimpse	czar	whençe	earl
wrench	daunt	wrist	learn
craunch	halve	wring	deaf
breath	gaunt	staunch	tough

2	4	3	3
trudge	gnash	wrought	prompt
grudge	gnat	fought	scorch
ridge	wool	naught	scrawl
writ	lose	warmth	mosque
wealth	scratch	cough	stalk
death	haunch	caught	taught
chintz	crash	trough	shalt

There are a great many fine nerves, and at the ends of the fingers the skin is quite thin, so that we may feel with them.

And then you have nails, to assist you in picking up small things.

If the nails were on the underside of the hand they would be in the way, and would soon wear off.

Nails are of great use to protect the ends both of fingers and toes.

3	4	1	2	3	32	33
nor,	good,—	tube,	tub,	bull,—	oil,	pound,—thin, THIS

2	2	1	3
who	struck	sieze	gorge
croup	through	lief	scotch
rouge	clutch	piece	groat
tour	fledge	poult	thought
whose	thence	fief	broad
loose	prove	yield	sought
tomb	whom	liege	fraud
move	soothe	forge	bought

1	33	33	33
thee	drowse	mouth	owl
thine	spouse	house	scowl
these	trounce	browse	doubt
those	flounce	shroud	drought
thy	growl	trout	doubt
the	ounce	mouths	sprout
oaths	plough	slouch	pounce
wreaths	crouch	mouse	bough

Come, let us go and see Jane milk the cow.

May we have some nice fresh milk!

Yes, you may.

Take your cup. She will fill it for you.

How still the cow stands.

The cow is a good friend to little boys and girls, as she gives them rich milk, which is the best food they can have.

| 1 | 2 | 3 | 4 | 1 | 2 | 1 | 2 | 1 | 2 |
fate, far, fall, fat,—me, met,—pine, pin,—no, move

33	32	32	32
lounge	choiçe	spoil	joined
bounçe	noiṣe	boil	quoif
pouçh	point	oint	quoin
ground	poiṣe	foist	coil
gout	broil	toils	groin
howl	voiçe	foils	hoit
spouṣe	moist	joint	moil
hound	hoist	joist	join

	1	1	2
pique*	sleave	buy	sweat
prey†	steak	sword	been
seine†	tier	choir§	drachm
sleigh†	threw	coarae	plumb
sew‡	thrown	corps	quilt
sley†	known	dough	built

* *i* sounded like *e*.   ‡ *ew* like *o*.
† *e* sounded like *a*.   § *ch* like *kw*.

Have you been to school today?

Yes sir.

Do you love your teacher?

Yes sir; because he is so very kind.

All my classmates love him too.

He seems so sorry when we do not know our lessons. We all strive to learn, that we may please him, and grow up to be wise men.

3   4   1   2   3   32   33
nor, good,—tube, tub, bull,—oil, pound,—thin, THIS

THE SEAL.

George Bliss was a good lad. His father one day gave him a new book, in which were pictures of birds and of fishes. He did not know what to think of the seal; "for" said he, "it does not look much like a fish, and I am quite sure it is not a bird. Do sir, tell me about it."

"A seal," said his father, "is in part like a beast, and in part like a fish. It can live both on land and in the sea; but it is most like a fish and seems to like best to live in the sea.

Its head is round like that of a man's. It has teeth like a dog's, and its eyes are large and bright. It has black hair which shines as if oil had been put on it.

Seals have four feet; but the two hind feet are very much like fins, and are of no use on land. They live on fish and are found in the north seas. They are killed for their skins, and the oil which their fat yields."

"But," said George, "why do the seals stay in that sad cold place, among the icebergs? They should swim south, where the water is warm."

1	2	3	4	1	2	1	2	1	2

fate, far, fall, fat,—me, met,—pine, pin,—no, move

"True, my son," said his father "but God has made them to love the cold climate they live in, and they would soon all die, if they should come south.

The seal, and the polar bear, and many other animals, live best where it is very cold. And if men and animals were not able to bear the cold, nearly one half of the earth would be of no use, and nothing could live there.

If the seal should come south, it would suffer with the heat, quite as much as we should, with the cold in the north. You might also ask the same question, about the men who live in the frozen zone, and whose life seems more miserable than that of the seals. God has wisely ordered, that every one should love his own country and climate above all others, and thus provided that on all parts of the globe, there should be both men and animals; and that both should enjoy life in the country where they are born.

Would you wish to go south, and live in the torrid zone? I suppose you will say "No!" But the people who live there, often wonder how we can endure so cold a climate; and are as unwilling as you, to change their place of living."

3	4	1	2	3	32	33

nor, good,—tube, tub, bull,—oil, pound,—thin, THIS

SECTION XXI.

Words of five syllables, accented on the second.

2	2	2	2	2

in dif' fer ent ly

in tel li ği ble

dis in ter est ed

in cor ri ği ble

2	2	2	2	2

in quis' i tive ly

in vid i ous ly

in el i ği ble

in tel li ğen çer

2	2	2	4	2

in vul ner a ble

in ex pli ca ble

in del i ca çy

in im it a ble

sig nif i ca tive

in çen di a ry

in term in a ble

sig nif i cant ly

2	2	2	4	2

in ev i ta ble

in es ti ma ble

im pen e tra ble

dis crim i na tive

il lit e ra cy

ef fem i na çy

in suf fer a ble

ad verb i al ly

Winter is very cold, but still it is pleasant.

See this new clean soft white snow, as it falls and hides the ground.

Now boys can made snowballs and have a great many kinds of sport in the snow.

When the sun shines warmly, the snow melts and sinks into the ground or runs into the brooks and rivers.

In the north part of Europe they sometimes have snow storms which smother whole flocks of sheep.

| 1 | 2 | 3 | 4 | 1 | 2 | 1 | 2 | 1 | 2 |

fate, far, fall, fat,—me, met,—pine, pin,—no, move

	1	2	2	4	2

he red' i ta ry

de lib er a tive

pre lim in a ry

de ġen er a çy

le ġit i ma çy

nu mer ic al ly

spe cif ic al ly

po et ic al ly

| 1 | 2 | 2 | 4 | 2 |

de lib er ate ly

de ġen' er ate ly

de term in a tive

he ret ic al ly

po lit i cal ly

le ġit i mate ly

pre cip i tan çy

de term in a ble

| 2 | 4 | 2 | 4 | 2 |

in hab it a ble

im prac ti ca ble

ġym nas tic al ly

dis pas sion ate ly

im aġ in a ry

pi rat ic al ly

| 4 | 1 | 2 | 2 | 2 |

gra tu i tous ly

ab ste mi ous ness

ap pro pri ate ly

la bor ri ous ly

ma te ri al ist

ab ste mi ous ly

Do you know how paper is made?

It is made from rags, and sometimes straw.

The paper we use to write on is always made from rags.

The rags are all scraped into pieces until they look like paste.

This paste or pulp is then spread into thin sheets which are dried and trimmed and prepared for use.

The paper used in stores, to tie up goods with, is made of straw or very coarse rags.

| 3 | 4 | 1 | 2 | 3 | 32 | 33 |
nor, good,—tube, tub, bull,—oil, pound,—thin, THIS

3 2

com par′ a tive ly
con fed er a çy
con sid er a ble
con sid er ate ly
com mem o ra tive
con tem po ra ry
con sid er a bly
com mem o ra ble

2 2 1

ir reg′ u lar ly
ir rev o ca ble
in val u a ble
in ex o ra ble
ri dic u lous ly
in dis so lu ble
im pen e tra ble
ex tem po ra ry

2 2 1

dis trib u tive ly
di min u tive ly
in dis so lu bly
ir rev o ca bly
in dis pu ta ble
par tic u lar ly
dis pens a to ry
in ex o ra ble

2 3 2

in vol un ta ry
in tol er a bly
in hos pi ta ble
in cor ri ġi ble
in for mi da ble
in or di na çy
in tol er a ble
sup poṣ it o ry

See these young birds; how they climb up on the edge of the nest.

Take care, little chirpers, or you will fall.

Ah! There comes their mother, as swift as an arrow, with a large fly in her mouth.

How they stretch their necks!

Poor things! They are very hungry.

Now look, and you may see the old bird feed them.

| 1 | 2 | 3 | 4 | 1 | 2 | 1 | 2 | 1 | 2 |
fate, far, fall, fat,—me, met,—pine, pin,—no, move

1 1 2 2 2
pre ca' ri ous ly
e gre gi ous ly

2
un gov' ern a ble*
un com fort a ble*

1 1 2 2 2
me lo di ous ly
la bo ri ous ly
pe nu ri ous ly
ma te ri al ly
no to ri ous ly

4 2
mag nif i çent ly
ca lum ni a tor
mag nan i mous ly
am big u ous ly
ac cus tom a ble

3 1
com mo di ous ly
com mu ni ca ble
con ve ni ent ly
op pro bri ous ly
con cu pis çen çy

1 2 1 4 2
co tem po ra ry
tu mult u a ry
vo lup tu a ry
re şid u a ry
de gen e ra çy

3 3 2 1 2
con sol a to ry
prog nos ti ca ting

1 2 2
vo lup tu ous ness
de gen er a ted

* In these words, o in the second syllable is pronounced like u in tub.

Soon these little nestlings will be able to fly and seek food for themselves. Then, as soon as it begins to grow cold in the fall they will fly away, far south, to remain until spring returns.

These birds are called martins.

Did you ever see a martin?

| 3 | 4 | | 1 | 2 | 3 | 32 | 33 |
nor, good,—tube, tub, bull,—oil, pound,—thin, THIS

SECTION XXII.

Words of five syllables, accented on the third.

2 2 2 2 2
in si pid' i ty
in di viş i ble
un in tel li ģent
in fi del i ty
in di viş i bly
viş i bil i ty

2 2 2 2 2
sens i bil' i ty
im per çept i ble
cred i bil i ty
flex i bil i ty
in sin çer i ty
in ex press i ble

2 1 1 2 2
in cre du li ty
per pe tu i ty
del e te ri ous
im pro pri e ty
im ma te ri al
im me mo ri al
sen a to ri al
in se cu ri ty

2 2 4 2 2
sim i lar i ty
lib er al i ty
ģen er al i ty
crim in al i ty
un in hab it ed
prin çi pal i ty
per ti naç i ty
çir cum am bi ent

The God that made earth and sea, made us and all things.

He is in Heaven, on earth and everywhere.

He sees all things.

He knows all things.

Night and day are the same to him.

He does not need light, to see; for he can read our hearts and tell every thought as soon as we can ourselves.

| 1 | 2 | 3 | 4 | 1 | 2 | 1 | 2 | 1 | 2 |
fate, far, fall, fat,—me, met,—pine, pin,—no, move

2 1 1 22
çer e mo′ ni al
dic ta to ri al
dis o be di ent
mul ti tu din ous
im pro pri e ty
çer e mo ni ous
dis a gree a ble
ir re triev a ble

2 2 1 2
ed i to′ ri al
as si du i ty
in ex pe di ent
in ex pe ri ençe
min is te ri al
per spi cu i ty
pres by te ri an
ter ri to ri al

3 2 1 2
con sen ta ne ous
con spi cu i ty
con ti gu i ty
lon ġi tu din al

1 2 2 22
u ni vers i ty
e qui lib ri um
re ca pit u late
e lec triç i ty

2 1 3 24
hyp o chon dri ac
phil o loġ ic al
phil o soph ic al

1 2 2 2 2
pu sil lan i mous
mu ta bil i ty
mu li eb ri ty

Jane Hall had a fine black hen, which she used to feed with crumbs, until she was quite tame.

One day this hen got out of the yard with her little chickens.

Jane soon missed her, and taking the dog, set off to hunt her, for she was afraid she might lose her chickens.

3	4	1	2	3	32	33
nor, good,—tube, tub, bull,—oil, pound,—thin, THIS

2   3

ex com mu′ ni cate
in con çeiv a ble
in con so la ble
in con sid er ate
in con test a ble
in cor rupt i ble
im por tu ni ty
in con ve ni ent

2   3

in com mo′ di ous
in con ve ni ençe
in con form i ty
im mor tal i ty
in con sist ent ly
in com pat i ble
dis con tent ed ly
in con dens a ble

4   1

an te çe dent ly
as tro nom ic al
caş u ist ic al
man u fac tur er′
math e mat ic al
cat e gor ic al
ab o riġ i neş
ap o the o sis

4   1

gland u lif er ous
as tro loġ ic al
man u fac to ry
al le gor ic al
val e dic to ry
ap pre hens i ble
gland u los i ty
ar e am e try

Soon they found the hen making a loud noise. She was trying to chase off a young fox cub that wanted to seize her chickens.

The dog soon killed the fox. The hen was so grateful, that she always went with the dog after that. She would sometimes roost in his kennel.

1	2	3	4	1	2	1	2	1	2

fate, far, fall, fat,—me, met,—pine, pin,—no, move

4   2

ac çi dent' al ly
an i mos i ty
an ni vers a ry
ar is toc ra cy
fal li bil i ty
taç i turn i ty
ac ri mo ni ous
am bi gu i ty

4   2

as si du' i ty
sanc ti mo ni ous
mat ri mo ni al
al i ment a ry
sat is fac to ry
am phi the a tre
pat ri mo ni al
quad ri lat er al

4   4

an a log ic al
an a lyt ic al
an a tom ic al
as a foet i da
mag na nim i ty
pla ca bil i ty
ac a dem ic al
am a to ri al

4   4

salv a bil i ty
an a mor pho sis
af fa bil i ty
ad van tage ous ly
cab a list ic al
par a dox i cal
par al lel o gram
par a lyt ic al

Some plants grow on steep rocks, where no man can climb; some in wet bogs, and some in deep shady forests.

How can the rose draw its crimson from the dark brown earth; or the lily its pure white?

He that made them is wiser than we.

He alone can tell.

```
 2   2  1   2    2
mul ti tu' din ous
in ex pe di ent
in ter ja çen çy
mer i to ri ous
mis çel la ne ous
per i cra ni um
in ex pe ri ençe
per spi cu i ty
```

```
 2    1   2    2    2
ir re vers' i ble
in de struct i ble
in sta bil i ty
ig no min i ous
rep re hens i ble
vers a til i ty
im be çil i ty
in tre pid i ty
```

```
 3        2   2 2
con san guin i ty
prob a bil i ty
pos si bil i ty
com pre hen si ble
```

```
 4  4   2    2  2
an a gram ma tist
car a van sa ry
sal va bil i ty
al pha bet ic al
```

We must fear God, and love him also. He is to be feared because he hates bad men, and bad acts. And he whom God hates cannot be happy. God must be loved because he loves us.

He feeds us and clothes us, and keeps watch over us night and day. God's eye never sleeps, but looks always at us. We cannot fly to anyplace where he cannot find us; nor hide in any place where he cannot see us.

Our friends, our food, our clothes; all we have, comes from His kind hand, which is never weary in doing us good.

| 1 | 2 | 3 | 4 | 1 | 2 | 1 | 2 | 1 | 2 |
fate, far, fall, fat,—me, met,—pine, pin,—no, move

SECTION XXIII.

Words of five syllables, accented on the fourth.

| 3 | 2 | 2 | 1 |
con fed er a' tion
com miş er a tion
ob lit er a tion
con çil i a tion

| 3 | 2 | 2 | 1 |
con sid er a' tion
mod i fi ca tion
con fig u ra tion
com mem o ra tion

| 4 | 2 | 2 | 1 |
ac çel er a tion
clar i fi ca tion
man i fest a tion
rat i fi ca tion
al lit er a tion
grat i fi ca tion
ad min is tra tion
am pli fi ca tion

| 4 | 2 | 2 | 1 |
an tiç i pa tion
ca lum ni a tion
an nun çi a tion
sanc ti fi ca tion
as sev er a tion
ad min is tra tor
ad min is tra trix
ad min is tra tion

Let us walk down to the bank of the river, and enjoy the cool air. How bright the clouds are, in the west. They all seem to have edges of gold.

When the sun gets a little lower, they will become white, and then quite dark; for it is the sun which gives them their beautiful hues.

But as the moon rises they will again brighten and smile in her light.

| 3 | 4 | 1 | 2 | 3 | 32 | 33 | |
nor, good,—tube, tub, bull,—oil, pound,—thin, THIS

PUSS AND HER KITTENS.

Here is Puss and her kittens. Puss is lying down. The kittens are playing about her. How many kittens has Puss? Let me see— one, two, three. How innocent the little things appear! When they are older they will catch mice. Some children are so wicked as to hurt little kittens. But we will not hurt our kittens. We will take good care of them. We will give them some milk to lap with their little tongues. Good children do not hurt any animals. Good children do not hurt each other. Oh, no! They take no pleasure in such things. Good children are kind. In this they are like God. He is kind to the evil and to the unthankful, and ever doing us good. Therefore little children should love one another. Did you ever learn that beautiful hymn which says,

"Let love through all your actions run,
  And all your words be mild?"

I hope you will learn it. It was written for little children, and may do you much good.

1	2	3	4	1	2	1	2	1	2

fate, far, fall, fat,—me, met,—pine, pin,—no, move

1   4   2   1

e man ci pa' tion
pre var i ca tion
re tal i a tion
co hab it a tion
di laç er a tion
pro cras ti na tion
de cap it a tion
e rad i ca tion

2   2   1   1

dis sim u la' tion
cir cum lo cu tion
in ter po la tion
in vig o ra tion
ges tic u la tion
ar tic u la tion
in ter ro ga tion
ac çent u a tion

2   2   1   1

ca pit u la tion
mis al le ga tion
in sin u a tion
in ter pre ta tion
per pet u a tion
ex ten u a tion
ma tric u la tion
as sev er a tion

2   2   2   1

ed i fi ca tion
vers i fi ca tion
in vest i ga tion
çiv il i za tion
dis crim in a tion
ex hil er a tion
ex term in a tion
fruc ti fi ca tion

How swiftly that steamboat glides along!
The water foams around her wheels. The fires
glow in her engines, and the white vapor
shoots up into the air, with a loud noise.

She comes, filled with the fruits of other
lands; the rich grape, and the pulpy orange.
The merchant sees her and is glad, for she
carries his wealth in her bosom.

3   4   1   2   3   32   33
nor, good,—tube, tub, bull,—oil, pound,—thin, THIS

2   2   2   1
mul ti pli ca' tion
jus ti fi ca tion
sig ni fi ca tion

2   2   2   1
viv i fi ca' tion
spec if i ca tion
in vest i ga tion

2   2   2   1
par tic i pa tion
sub til i za tion
im ag in a tion
ter ĝi ver sa tion

3   4   1
con cat e na tion
con fab u la tion
con grat u la tion
or gan i za tion

1 3   1
co op e ra tion
de nom i na tion
de pop u la tion
de com po si tion

1   1
ne go ti a tion
e lu çi da tion
hi e ro glyph ic
ne go ti a tor

3   3   1
cor rob o ra tion
con sol i da tion
prog nos tic a tion

1   1
re mu ner a tion
re cu per a tion
e lu tri a tion

Now the boat has reached the wharf.

See how the crowd gathers around her.

Friend meets friend, and the cordial grasp of the hand, and the kindly greeting are exchanged.

How rapidly the workers carry off the boxes, as they are put on shore!

The boat will soon be ready to start again.

Did you ever travel on a steamboat?

1	2	3	4	1	2	1	2	1	2
fate,	far,	fall,	fat,—	me,	met,—	pine,	pin,—	no,	move

SECTION XXIV.

Words of six syllables, accented on the fourth.

2 2 2 2 2 2
dis sim i lar' i ty
el i ği bil i ty
di viş i bil i ty
sus çep ti bil i ty

2 3 2 2 2
im pos si bil' i ty
im prob a bil i ty
in con tro vert i ble
in com pre hens i ble

2 2 2 2 2
in cred i bil i ty
in sen si bil i ty
in viş i bil i ty
in flex i bil i ty
per çep ti bil i ty
ex per i ment al ly

1 1
su pe ri or i ty
pe cu li ar i ty
me te or ol o ğy
a be çe da ri an
ma te ri al i ty
im mu ta bil i ty

2 2 2 2 2
mu nic i pal i ty
dis çi plin a ri an

2 1 2
in ca pa bil i ty
en thu şi ast ic al

Hark! The town clock strikes. One, two, three. The bell must be very large and the hammer quite heavy, or we could not hear it so far.

Clocks have weights to move them, and watches have springs. Did you ever see the main spring of a watch?

We will go to the Silversmith's, and perhaps he will be so kind as to show you one.

3   4   1   2   3   32   33
nor, good,—tube, tub, bull,—oil, pound,—thin, THIS

2   2   1

het er o ge′ ne ous
im pet u os i ty
ir reg u lar i ty
ex tem po ra ne ous
çir cum fo ra ne ous
ir rep re hen si ble
sem i di am e ter
un çer e mo ni ous

4   2

am bi dex ter i ty
prac ti ca bil i ty
ac çept a bil i ty
par a di și a cal
an ti mo narch i cal
ar is to crat i cal
ad min is tra tor ship
ar chi e pis co pal

2   4

in fal li bil i ty
dis sat is fac to ry
im pas si bil i ty
im palp a bil i ty

1   2

me di a to ri al
mu ni çi pal i ty
pre des ti na ri an
re șist i bil i ty

1   2

pu sil lan im i ty
u ni ver sal i ty
su per a bun dant ly

1   2

re flex i bil i ty
su per in tend en çy
re spect a bil i ty

This spring is made of fine steel, and is coiled up in a little brass box. When the watch is wound, the spring is drawn tight.

It is strong enough to move all the wheels. One hand of the watch moves fast, to tell us the minutes; the short hand points out the hour.

The long hand, is called the minute hand, and moves twelve times as fast as the other.

| 1 | 2 | 3 | 4 | 1 | 2 | 1 | 2 | 1 | 2 |

fate, far, fall, fat,—me, met,—pine, pin,—no, move

SECTION XXV.

In this Section, *i*, when in an unaccented syllable and followed by a vowel has the power of a consonant and the sound of *y*.

1 2	4	1 2
al' ien	pann ier	do min ion
al ien ate	pa vil ion	mo dill ion
2 2	gal iot	o pin ion
bil ious	2	re bell ion
2 4	bill ion	de duc tion
fil ial	min ion	4 4
triv ial	pin ion	bat tal ion
ruff ian	scull ion	ras cal ion
brill iant	mill ion	4 2 4
3 2	trunn ion	con viv ial
pon iard	trill ion	fa mil iar

"Pa!" said James Wake "how do we know that there is a God who takes care of us?"

"If you should find a watch," said his father "would you not suppose that someone had made it?"

"Yes sir," said James.

"Then," said his papa "if we see every day around us a great many things more perfect than a watch, must we not think that they too have been made?"

"Certainly," said James.

3	4	1	2	3	32	33

nor, good,—tube, tub, bull,—oil, pound,—thin, THIS

SECTION XXVI.

In this Section, *t*, has the sound of *tsh* when immediately followed by *u*.

1 1	2 1	2 1 2
crea' ture	sculp' ture	sump' tu ous
na ture	rup ture	çen tu ry
fu ture	stric ture	gut tu ral
fea ture	ges ture	fis tu lous
su ture	4 1	cour te ous
2 1	stat ure	2 2 4
nur ture	stat ue	bes ti al
tex ture	stat ute	4 1 1
ves ture	3 1	ac tu ate
lec ture	for tune	grat u late
mix ture	2 4	2 4 1
vul ture	fus tian	curv a ture

"Now," said his papa "in every blade of grass there is more to admire than in anything which man can make.

Its maker then must be wiser than we are.

The grass could not happen to be as it is, any more than the watch.

And if we admire the skill of the watchmaker, we should much more admire the wisdom of God, who has done all things well.

How happy are they who have this wise and great God, for their friend.

1	2	3	4		1	2		1	2		1	2
fate, far, fall, fat,—me, met,—pine, pin,—no, move

2 1	4 1	2 1
scrip ture	frac' ture	çen' tu ry
fix ture	cap ture	fluc tu ate
ven ture	rap ture	fur ni ture
cul ture	pas ture	pet u lançe
pus tule	3 1	rit u al
ven ture	pos ture	pet u lant
pic ture	33	33
struc ture	joint ed	boun te ous

2 3 1	4 1 4 2	1 2 2 2
mis for' tune	ac' tu al ly	pre sump tu ous
im pos ture	ac tu a ry	tu mult u ous
4 2 1	nat u ral ist	vo lup tu ous
ad ven ture	grat u la ry	3 2 1
3 2 1	stat u a ry	con jec' tur al
con tex ture	nat u ral ly	con stit u ent
con jec ture	1 1 4 2	con tempt u ous
com mix ture	mu tu al ly	con grat u late

James and Jane go to the same school.

They learn to read and write and sing.

How pleasant it is to hear children sing together. Can you sing?

If you cannot, you must make haste and learn.

It will be sweet to mingle your young voices in a song or hymn, around your father's fireside.

3	4	1	2	3	32	33

nor, good,—tube, tub, bull,—oil, pound,—thin, THIS

SECTION XXVII.

In this section, c, s, and t have the sound of *sh*, when immediately followed by *i* or *u*.

2 1	4 2	1 2 1
çen' sure	tran' şient	pro pi' tiate
pres sure	1 4	li çen tiate
tis su*e*	gla' çial	e nun ciate
1 1	3 1 4	no vi tiate
spe' çies	con' su lar	2 1 1
1 1	4 4	ex pa' tiate
gla' çiate	caş' şia	in gra tiate
ra tio	2 2 1	in sa tiate
sa tiate	in i' tiate	2 21
1 2	1 1	vi ti a' tion
pre' scient	as so' çiate	4 2 1
pre scien*ç*e	dis so çiate	of fi' çiate

When the bright sun sets in the evening it is soon dark.

The birds cease their songs and go to sleep with their heads behind their wings.

The busy streets of the great city and the green field are alike; still.

The great sun has gone to shine upon another part of the world and the bright stars are seen in the sky. Here and there a cloud is seen, whitened by the light of the new moon.

1	2	3	4	1	2	1	2	1	2

fate, far, fall, fat,—me, met,—pine, pin,—no, move

SECTION XXVIII.

In the last syllable of the following words *s* and *z* have the sound of *zh*, and the vowel which is not silent has the short sound of *u*.

1
fu' sion
ho sier
o sier
gla zier
gra zier
1 1
co he' sion
de lu sion
e va sion
pro fu sion
4 1
al lu sion
a bra sion
af fu sion
ad he sion

3 1
col lu' sion
con clu sion
con fu sion
cor ro sion
oc ca sion
con tu sion
1 2
de ri sion
re vi sion
pro vi sion
de çi sion
re çi sion
e li sion
pre çi sion
se çes sion

2 1
dif fu' sion
suf fu sion
per sua sion
dis clo sure
ef fu sion
dis plo sion
in va sion
il lu sion
in fu sion
ex po sure
ex plo sion
2 2
di vi sion
mis pri sion
in çi sion

Before all lands in east or west,
I love my native land the best,
    With God's best gifts 'tis teeming.
No gold or jewels here are found,
But men of noble souls abound,
    And eyes with joy are beaming.

3	4	1	2	3	32	33

nor, good,—tube, tub, bull,—oil, pound,—thin, THIS

SECTION XXIX.

In the following words, *i* in the final syllables has the sound of *ee*.

	4	2 2
frize	an tique'	ver' di gris
shire	ca priçe	4 4
1	cha grin	gab ar dine'
po lice'	fa tigue	man da rin
pro file	ma chine	tam bou rine
pe lisse	ma rine	mag a zine

And now my dear little boys and girls, this is the last reading lesson in the Eclectic Spelling Book.

If you have been attentive, you will now be able to use the First Reader. But if you have not, it would be better for you to spend a few more weeks in this book.

If you leave the Speller too soon, you will be much longer in learning to read well, than if you had not been in such a hurry.

I hope you have kept all your books quite clean and nice, so that you will love to use them. But we sometimes get tired of old books; so if your teacher pleases, you shall now have a new one.

1	2	3	4	1	2	1	2	1	2
fate,	far,	fall,	fat,—	me,	met,—	pine,	pin,—	no,	move

SECTION XXX.

In the following words *e* is silent in the last syllable.

1	3	32
fa' çed	lodg' ed	oil' ed
gra çed	solv ed	coil ed
la çed	warm ed	boil ed
tra çed	warp ed	broil ed
pa çed	warn ed	toil ed
bra çed	scorn ed	soil ed
scra ped	call ed	foil ed
bla zed	haul ed	**33**
cri ed	maul ed	bow ed
drain ed	gall ed	rouş ed
fear ed	**4**	drown ed
flow ed	laugh ed	crown ed
hail ed	mark ed	scour ed
la med	charm ed	sour ed
sa ved	class ed	frown ed
na med	crack ed	plaw ed
rain ed	dash ed	**4 1**
raiş ed	flash ed	a bu' şed
su ed	pass ed	ac cu şed
pa ved	**2**	ac qui red
tu ned	beg ged	ad mi red
roll ed	liv ed	at ti red
snow ed	rub bed	a do red
crow ed	prov ed	ad vi şed
mow ed	mov ed	a mu şed

3   4   1   2   3   32   33
nor, good,—tube, tub, bull,—oil, pound,—thin, THIS

1 2	2 2	3 1
re volv′ ed	ex pun′ ged	com bi′ ned
e volv ed	in frin ged	com mu ned
de form ed	sub serv ed	con su med
de volv ed	dis charg ed	con ve ned
re call ed	en larg ed	con troll ed
1 2	em bark ed	con sol ed
di vul ged	ex press ed	con fuṣ ed
re turn ed	dis miss ed	2 2
re veng ed	im press ed	op press ed
1 1	dis pens ed	con fess ed
be liev ed	dis pers ed	con vin çed
re liev ed	sup press ed	2 3
be sieg ed	2 1	dis solv ed
be reav ed	en ti çed	in volv ed
de fa med	dis gra çed	in stall ed
re vi led	di vor çed	1 33
de pri ved	e sca ped	de noun çed
4 1	im peach ed	re noun çed
blas phe med	in creas ed	de vour ed
chas ti ṣed	in du çed	pro noun çed
bap ti zed	en roll ed	2 32
ar ri ved	ex cuṣ ed	em ploy ed
as cri bed	en gross ed	en joy ed
a vail ed	em bra çed	4 4
as sail ed	en for çed	ad van çed
ap pear ed	dis pla çed	at tack ed
a ba sed	en tail ed	a larm ed

1	2	3	4	1	2	1	2	1	2

fate, far, fall, fat,—me, met,—pine, pin,—no, move

SECTION XXXI.

Words in which *ch* has the power of *k*.

1 4
li' lach
cho ral
 1 2
cho rus
te trarch
 2 2
dis tich
chem ist
christ en
pyr rich
 3 2
schol ar
chol er
chol ic
mon arch
 1 1
tro chee
 4 2
cham brel
mas tich
 4 4
pas chal
an arch
 1 3
cha os

4 4
bac' cha nals
an ar chy
char ac ter
sac cha rine
4 2
arch i tect
arch i trave
harp si chord
al che mist
ca chex y
lach ry mal
mach i nate
 2 2
christ en ing
chem ic al
christ en dom
tech nic al
chem is try
chrys a lis
 1 4
me chan' ic
scho las tic
chro mat ic
 3 2
mon' arch y

1 3
chi rog' ra phy
chi rog ra pher
psy chol o gy
chro nol o gy
chro nom e ter
chro nol o gist
 3 3
lo gom a chy
lo gom a chist
mo nom a chy
 2 3
ich nog ra phy
 4 1
cat e chu' men
cat e chet i cal
 1 4
eu cha ris' ti cal
 1 1
psy cho log i cal
 1 1
hi' e rar chy
 2 2
chi mer' ic al
 2 4
mel' an chol y

3	4	1	2	3	32	33

nor, good,—tube, tub, bull,—oil, pound,—thin, THIS

SECTION XXXII.

In the following words *x* has its flat sound like *gz* when it occurs in an unaccented syllable, and the next letter is a vowel or *h* mute.

2 1	2 2	2 1
ex hale'	ex er çent	lux u' ri ançe
ex ile'	ex em plar	ex u be rançe
ex ude	ex hib it	lux u ri ate
2 2	ex ist ent	ex u vi al
ex ist	ex er tion	ex u ber ant
ex act	**2 4 2**	ex il ing
ex em*p*t	ex am' ple	ex ha la ble
ex ult	ex act ed	**2 3**
ex ert	ex act ness	ex or di um
ex er*gue*	ex ot ic	ex or bi tant
2 3	**2 4 2**	ex or bi tançe
ex *h*ort	ex act' er	ex on er ate
ex *h*au*st*	ex am in*e*	ex ec u trix
ex alt	ex act ly	**2 2 1**
2 4	**2 1**	ex ig u *o*us
ex act	ex *h*ale ment	ex ec u tor
2 2	ex ile ment	ex ec u tive
ex emp' tion	ex u be rate	ex an i mate

1	2	3	4	1	2	1	2	1	2

fate, far, fall, fat,—me, met,—pine, pin,—no, move

SECTION XXXIII.

Anomalies in pronunciation.

Written	Pronounced	Written	Pronounced
buoy	boue (33)	hic cough	hĭk' hup (2)
choir	kwire (1)	laugh ter	laf' tur (2)
cough	kof (3)	ma ny	men' ne (2 2)
clerk	klark (2)	neph ew	nev' vu (2 1)
compt	kount (33)	pret ty	prit te (2)
draught	draft (2)	waist coat	wes' kot (2)
laugh	laf (2)	ser geant	sar' jant (2)
one	wun (2)	su gar	shu' gur (1)
once	wuns (2)	wom en	wim' min (2 2)
pique	peek (1)	a gain	a gen' (2)
rouge	roozhe (2)	a gainst	a genst' (2)
says	sez (2)	bat teau	bat to' (1)
said	sed (2)	bu reau	bu' ro (1 1)
slough	sluff (2)	cri tique	kre teek'
tough	tuff (2)	co quette	ko ket' (1 2)
trough	trof (3)	der nier	dern yare' (2 1)
a ny	en' ne (2 1)	e nough	e nuf' (2 1)
a pron	a' purn (1 2)	main tain	men tane' (2 1)
ax iom	ak' shum (1)	ron deau	ron do' (3 1)
busi ness	biz' ness (2 2)	chor is ter	kwir' is tur (2 2)
bu sy	biz' ze (2 1)	hal le lu jah	halle loo' ya (2)
colo nel	kur' nel (2 2)	lieu ten ant	lu ten' nant (1 2)
cup board	kub' burd	port man teau	port man' to (1)
flam beau	flam' bo (1)	pal an quin	pal an keen'
i ron	i' urn (1)	roq ue laur	rok' e lor (1)

3	4		1	2	3	32	33	

nor, good,—tube, tub, bull,—oil, pound,—thin, THIS

SECTION XXXIV.

Geographical proper names.

1	1	1	1
Ayr	Drave	Hague	Prgue
Spain	Tay	Trave	Wales
Zaire	Thames	Crete	Dee
Leeds	Treves	Thebes	Lieth
Nile	Tyne	Rhine	Schweitz
Rhone	Rhodes	Soane	Rome
2	**2**	**2**	**2**
Ghent	Hartz	Berne	Fez
Nyd	Perth	Trent	Ems
Ouse	Scheldt	Hull	Mentz
3	**3**	**3**	**3**
York	Cork	Thorn	Knox
Gaul	Ghauts	Dahl	Borgne
Pskov	Don	Tomsk	Dort
4	**4**	**4**	**4**
Bath	Zante	Nantes	Stantz
Gratz	France	Alps	Ban
1	**1**	**1**	**1**
A' ral	A' von	A' zoph	A' thos
Cai ro	Na ples	Ca diz	Cam bridge
Na tick	Pa ros	Sa lem	Ta gus
Pha ros	E den	East ham	Green land
Le high	Swe den	Bre men	De los
Dnie per	Dnie ster	E rie	Fried land
Fries land	He brus	Je na	Le man

1	2	3	4	1	2	1	2	1	2
fate,	far,	fall,	fat,—me,	met,—pine,	pin,—no,	move

1

1	1	1
We' ser	Wheel' ing	Guyş' burg
Di*gh* ton	Dwi na	I da
Fry*e* burg	*E*y der	Xi no
Ti gris	Ti ber	T*h*i bet
Ni phon	Do ver	Go shen
Port land	Gro ton	C*h*ro nus
Co mo	Go tham	Mo *ch*a
Ho reb	O by	O phir
Cu ba	C*e*u ta	Du ro
Hu ron	N*e*w port	N*e*w burg
N*e*w bern	U ral	Mu ni*ch*
Tru ro	Xu car	Ju ra

2

2	2	2
Par ma	Spar ta	Car mel
Mar lo*w*	Hart ford	Bar ca
Ar gos	Dart m*ou*th	Ar ma*gh*
Ha*e*r lem	Har vard	Par ma

2

2	2	2
Ber lin	Ber ģen	Bed ford
Chel s*ea*	Ches*h* ir*e*	Del hi
Den mark	Dept ford	Es sex
Per ry	Tren ton	West port
Et na	Ep som	El ba
Hec la	Krem lin	Len ox
Tex el	Shet land	Wet ter
Ven i*ç*e	Mel roşe	Mer çer
Leş bos	Jed do	Mec ca

3	4	1	2	3	32	33

nor, good,—tube, tub, bull,—oil, pound,—thin, THIS

2	2	2
Bridge' port	Bris' tol	Fish' kill
Lis bon	Litch field	Pitts burg
Pitts field	Plym outh	Wind ham
Rip ley	Syd ney	Quin çy
In spruck	Ips wich	Pin dus
Is sus	Guild hall	Bour bon
Coo sa	Brook lyn	Trux ton
Dur ham	Flush ing	Hunts ville
Hurl gate	Lud low	Bis cay

2	2	2
Pult ney	Rut land	Suf folk
Suf field	Sut ton	Uls ter
Hum ber	Stutt gard	Pul tusk
Cher burg	Prus sia	Sun da

3	3	3
Al ton	Balls ton	Dal ton
Au burn	Al ford	War saw
Bal tic	Cra cow	Falk land
Mal den	War wick	Ra leigh
Wal tham	York town	York shire

3	3	3
Wa bash	Wal ton	Corn wall
Nor way	Or leans	Bos ton
Lock port	Ox ford	Or ange
Stock port	Con cord	Con go
Gos port	Drontheim	Grod no
Ork ney	Goth land	Nor wich

1	2	3	4	1	2	1	2	1	2

fate, far, fall, fat,—me, met,—pine, pin,—no, move

3

Scot' land
Onș low

3

Shrop' shire
Ok kak

3

Wol' ga
Os sa

4

Taun' ton
Cam den
Dan ville
Ham den
Bag dat
Had dam
Straș burg
Nat çhez

4

Ac' ton
Cas co
Camp bell
Graf ton
Stam ford
Ham burg
Stral sund
Pat ras

4

Am' herst
Can ton
Chat ham
Hamp ton
Strat ford
Jack son
Rad nor
Platts burg

Accented on the second syllable.

1

Lou vain' Bom bay' Kil dare' O sage'
Tour nay Lo thain Dun dee Al giers
Dun frieș Mau mee San tee Pe dee
Tan gier Car lisle Pi qua Pe ru

2

Na varre' Oz ark' Lu çerne' Que bec'
Ro çhelle So relle Ver gennes Vin çennes
Ma drid Se ville Tou loușe Ya zoo

3

O kotsk' Al torf' Leg horn' Ban gor'
Cey lon Di jon To bolsk Ben gal

4

Bel fast' Su rat' Mi lan' Ma dras'

3	4	1	2	3	32	33

nor, good,—tube, tub, bull,—oil, pound,—thin, THIS

Accented on the first syllable.

1	1	1
Da' ri en	Ha' dri a	Ba' kers field
Fay ette ville	Pe ters burg	Green cas tle
Bla dens burg	Xe ni a	Ne gro pont
Hei del burg	Bo ling broke	Mo de na
Sto ning ton	Po co moke	Bu cha rest
Ru bi con	U ti ca	New ber ry
Lou is burg	Steu ben ville	Lew is town

2	2	2
Ar' ling ton	Barn' sta ble	Car' ters ville
Far ming ton	Mar tins ville	Marl bor ough
Bev er ly	Ben ning ton	Chel ten ham
Cel e beş	Ed in burg	Hel i con

2	2	2
Lex' ing ton	Mex' i co	Mer' ri mack
Thes sa ly	Ten e dos	Bev er ly
Ger man town	Ex e ter	Fred e rick
Jef fer son	Leb a non	Pen ning ton
Her ki mer	West ches ter	Lich ten au
Mid dle burg	Mid dle sex	Mid dle town
Win ches ter	Hills bor ough	In ver ness
It a ly	Ith a ca	Iv i ca
Lim er ick	Siçi ly	Vis tu la
Win ni peg	Hun ga ry	Lux em burg
Tus ca ny	Cum ber land	Bur ling ton
Buf fa lo	Dun sta ble	Cum ming ton

| 1 | 2 | 3 | 4 | 1 | 2 | 1 | 2 | 1 | 2 |

fate, far, fall, fat,—me, met,—pine, pin,—no, move

3	3	3
Wa' ter ford	Bal' ti more	Al' ba ny
Aus ter litz	Aus tri a	Wal sing ham
Bor ne o	Col ches ter	Got ten burg
Gron in gen	Os na burg	Cor si ca
Rox bu ry	Rot ter dam	Dor ches ter
Both ni a	Cov ing ton	Got tin gen

4	4	4
Am' a zon	Rar' i tan	Shafts' bu ry
Pam li co	Can a da	Hal i fax
Man ches ter	Dan bu ry	Ac ti um

Accented on the second syllable.

1	1	1
Ba ha' ma	Be na' res	Ja mai' ca
Pas sa ic	A ba ca	West pha lia
Cri me a	Ge ne va	Os we go
Ot se go	Co re a	Chal de a
Hel ve tia	Mo re a	To le do
Sa bri na	O hi o	Ce ri go
Me di na	Sa li na	An go la
Bas so ra	Co mo ra	Eu ro tas
Na po li	O co nee	Pe cho ra
Sci o to	Ti o ga	Ve ro na
La do ga	A zo res	Au ro ra
Ber mu das	Cay u ga	Hon du ras
Carls cro na	Cho lu la	Pal my ra

3   4   1   2   3   32 33
nor, good,—tube, tub, bull,—oil, pound,—thin, THIS

2	2	2
Caer nar' von	Sag har' bor	Lo ret' to
New Jer sey	Vi en na	Tom big bee
Pa ler mo	A ver nus	Kil ken ny
Sa ler num	Spitz ber gen	An til leş
La ris sa	Sar din ia	Ma nil la
Co im bra	Mus king um	Mo luc ca
Co lum bus	Nan tuck et	Oak mul ğee
Pa tuck et	New Bruns wick	San dus ky
Cal cut ta	Co lum bo	O lym pus

3	3	3
Gib ral' tar	Ken ha' wa	St. Law' rençe
Ma jor ca	New Or leaņs	Pe tor ca
Mi nor ca	Gol con da	Mo roc co
Pe nob scot	Ouis con sin	Hock hock ing

4	4	4
Ha va na	Co has set	Man hat tan
Pa taps co	Sa van nah	Wis cas set
Mi am i	Le pan to	North amp ton
Hy das pes	Ve nan go	Par nas sus

SECTION XXXV.

Proper names of persons.

1	1	2	4
Hugh	Ju' dith	Her od	Mat' thew
Giles	Lu çy	Fes tus	Sam son
Jane	Lu ther	Ed win	Ab ner
Luke	Su san	Ed ward	Al içe
James	Ti tus	Ez ra	Cal vin

1	2	3	4	1	2	1	2	1	2

fate, far, fall, fat,—me, met,—pine, pin,—no, move

1	1	2	4
Jude	Le' vi	Jus' tus	Fran çes
Ruth	Ly man	Leon ard	Han nah
Job	Si mon	Rich ard	Nan çy
Miles	Lew is	Eg bert	Sal ly
2	Mo ses	Den nis	**1**
Charles	Pe ter	Hen ry	Da ri' us
Mark	Jo el	El len	E li as
Clark	Jo nah	Em ma	E li sha
Seth	Sa rah	Hum phrey	Jo si ah
3	Mi chael	Wil liam	U ri ah
John	Pe rez	Es ther	E li zur
George	E noch	Ed gar	A bi el
Paul	Cae şar	**3**	A bi jah
Saul	Ma ry	Rob ert	E li za
4	Mi ra	Lau ra	So phi a
Ralph	Phe be	Hor açe	To bi as
1	Pi late	Wal ter	Ma ri a
Aa' ron	Ra chel	Thom as	**2**
A mos	Ne ro	Dor cas	Ma til da
A saph	Reu ben	God frey	Myr til la
Da vid	Ste phen	**4**	Be lin da
Ca leb	Ru fus	Al bert	Re bec ca
A bram	Si las	Al fred	Lo ren zo
Ba lak	**2**	Al len	Cla ris sa
Bo oz	Jes se	Al vin	Lu çin da
Flo ra	Mar cus	Dan iel	Au gus tus
Ja bez	Phil ip	An drew	Me lis sa

SECTION XXXVI.

*Quotations from other languages, which are
frequently used in English.*

Ab initio,	*L**	*From the beginning.*
Ad libitum	"	*At pleasure.*
Ad infinitum	"	*Without limits.*
Ad valorem	"	*According to value.*
A fortiori	"	*For stronger reason.*
Alma mater	"	*A cherishing mother†*
Anglice	"	*In English.*
Anno Domini	"	*The year of our Lord.*
Apriori	"	*From cause to effect.*
Anno Mundi	"	*The year of the world.*
Beaux Esprits, (boze espree) *F.*		*Men of wit.*
Beau Monde, (bo mond) *F.*		*The fashionable world.*
Bona Fide, *L.*		*In good faith.*
Bon mot, (bong mo) *F.*		*A witty saying.*
Bon ton, (bong tong) *F.*		*Fashion.*
Caput mortuum. *L.*		*The lifeless remains.*
Carte blanche, (cart blansh) *F.*		*Unconditional terms.*
Cap a pie, *F.*		*From head to foot.*
Coup d'oeil, (Coo dile) *F.*		*A glance.*
Coup de grace, (coo-d grase) *F.*		*Finishing stroke.*
Con amore, *L.*		*With love.*
Chief d'oeuvre, (shay devr) *F.*		*Masterpiece.*
Compos mentis, *L.*		*Of sound mind.*
Coup de main, (coop de main) *F.*		*A bold effort.*
Charge d'affaires, (sharzh daffare) *F.*		*A public messenger.*
Double entendre, (doob lantandr,) *F.*		*Capable of two interpretations.*
De novo, *L.*		*Anew.*
Dramatis personae, *L.*		*Persons represented.*
Ecce homo, *L.*		*Behold the man.*
En masse, (an mas) *F.*		*In a body, all together*

---

* *L.* signifies Latin, *F.* French &c.
† Applied to the college where one is educated.

E pluribus unum, *L.*	*One of many; motto to U.S.*
Ex officio, *L.*	*By virtue of office.*
Ex parte, *L.*	*On one side.*
Et caetera, *L.*	*And so forth.*
En passant, (ong passong)*F.*	*By the way.*
Fac simile, *L.*	*A close imitation.*
Faux pas, (fo pa) *F.*	*A false step.*
Felo de se, *L.*	*A self murderer.*
Fille de chambre, (feeld shambr) *F.*	*A chambermaid.*
Fortiter in re, *L.*	*Firm in action.*
Gens d'armes, (zhan darm) *F.*	*Police soldiers.*
Habeas corpus, *L.*	*You may have the body.*
Hic jacet, *L.*	*Here lies.*
Hors de combat, (hore de combat) *F.*	*Not in condition to fight.*
In statu quo, *L.*	*In the state in which it was.*
Ignis fatuus, *L.*	*A delusive light.*
In toto, *L.*	*In the whole.*
Ipse dixit,	*A bare assertion.*
Ipso facto, *L.*	*By that act.*
Jeu de mot, (zhu de mo) *F.*	*Play upon words.*
Jeu d'esprit, (zhu despree)*F.*	*A witticism.*
Jure divino, *L.*	*By divine right.*
Jus gentium, *L.*	*The law of nations.*
Lex talionis, *L.*	*The law of retaliation.*
Literatim, *L.*	*Letter for letter.*
Magna charta, *L.*	*The great charter.*
Malum in se, *L.*	*An evil in itself.*
Malapropos, (malapropo) *F.*	*Unsuitable.*
Memento mori, *F.*	*Forget not death.*
Minimum, *L.*	*The smallest.*
Mirabile dictu, *L.*	*Wonderful to tell.*
Multum in parvo, *L.*	*Much in little.*
Ne plus ultra, *L.*	*Nothing beyond.*
Nolens volens, *L.*	*Willing or unwilling.*
Non compos mentis, *L.*	*Insane.*
Pater patriae, *L.*	*Father of his Country.*
Per annum, *L.*	*By the year.*

Per diem, *L.*	*By the day.*
Petit maitre, (petty mater) *F.*	*A fop.*
Prima facie, *L.*	*On the first face.*
Primum mobile, *L.*	*The cause of motion.*
Pro bono publico, *L.*	*For public good.*
Pro tempore, *L.*	*For the time.*
Quantum, ? *L.*	*How much.*
Quantum sufficit, *L.*	*As much as is necessary.*
Quid nunc? *L.*	*What now? A newsmonger.*
Qui vive, (ke veov) *F.*	*The alert.*
Sanctum sanctorum, *L.*	*The most holy place.*
Sang froid, (sang froa) *L.*	*Indifference.*
Secundem artem,	*According to art.*
Sui generis, *L.*	*Of a peculiar kind.*
Sine die, *L.*	*No day agreed upon.*
Sine qua non, *L.*	*A thing indispensable.*
Soi disant, (swa dezan) *F.*	*Self styled.*
Summum bonum, *L.*	*The chief good.*
Sub rosa, *L.*	*Privately.*
Te Deum, *L.*	*A hymn of praise.*
Toties quoties, *L.*	*As many times as.*
Utile dulce, *L.*	*The useful with the agreeable.*
Ultimatum, *L.*	*The last offer.*
Valet de chambre, (valad shambr) *F.*	*A servant.*
Veto, *L.*	*A prohibition.*
Verbatim, *L.*	*Word for word.*
Veni, vidi, vici, *L.*	*I came, I saw, I conquered.*
Versus, *L.*	*Against.*
Via, *L.*	*By the way of.*
Vice, *L.*	*In the room of.*
Vice versa, *L.*	*The terms being reversed.*
Viva voce, *L.*	*With the living voice.*
Vive le roi, (veev lu roa) *F.*	*Long live the king.*

NOTE.—In Latin words, there is a syllable for every vowel, except in case of diphthongs. (Ex. vi va vo ce.)

1	2	3	4	1	2	1	2	1	2

fate, far, fall, fat,—me, met,—pine, pin,—no, move

SECTION XXXVII.

Words of which there are two or more of the same pronunciation, but of different orthography and signification.

1

Air, *an element.*
Ere, *before.*
Heir, *he who inherits.*
　Ail, *to be sick*
　Ale, *a malt liquor*
Bare, *naked.*
Bear, *to suffer.*
　Beet, *a vegetable.*
　Beat, *to strike.*
Bee, *an insect.*
Be, *to exist.*
　Blue, *a color.*
　Blew, *did blow.*
Bow, *to shoot with.*
Beau, *a suitor.*
　Bore, *to make a hole.*
　Boar, *a beast.*
Base, *low vile.*
Bass, *a part in music.*
　Bale, *a pack of goods.*
　Bail, *surety.*
Buy, *to purchase.*
By, *near.*
　Borne, *carried.*
　Bourn, *a limit.*
Coarse, *not fine.*
Course, *a race way.*
　Cote, *a sheep-fold.*
　Coat, *a garment.*

1

Core, *the heart.*
Corps, *a body of soldiers.*
　Clime, *a region*
　Climb, *to ascend.*
Deer, *an animal.*
Dear, *costly.*
　Fare, *provision.*
　Fair, *beautiful.*
Flee, *to run away.*
Flea, *an insect.*
　Fane, *a temple.*
　Fain, *gladly.*
　Feign, *to dissemble.*
Freeze, *to congeal.*
Frieze, *coarse cloth.*
　Grate, *for coals.*
　Great, *large.*
Hare, *an animal.*
Hair, *of the head.*
　Heel, *part of the foot.*
　Heal, *to cure.*
Here, *in this place.*
Hear, *to hearken.*
　Hue, *color.*
　Hew, *to cut.*
Hole, *a cavity.*
Whole, *total.*
　High, *lofty.*
　Hie, *to hasten.*

1

I, *myself.*
Eye, *organ of sight.*
Meet, *to assemble.*
Meat, *food.*
Mete, *to measure.*
Key, *an instrument.*
Quay, *a wharf.*
Leek, *an herb.*
Leak, *to run out.*
Leaf, *part of a plant.*
Lief, *willingly.*
Lyre, *a harp.*
Li-ar, *one who tells lies.*
Lone, *single.*
Loan, *anything lent.*
Mean, *low.*
Mien, *manner.*
Moan, *lament.*
Mown, *cut down.*
Nave, *part of a wheel.*
Knave, *a dishonest man.*
New, *not worn.*
Knew, *did know.*
Ore, *metal.*
Oar, *a thing to row with.*
Pane, *a square of glass.*
Pain, *uneasiness.*
Pare, *to cut off.*
Pair, *a couple.*
Pear, *a fruit.*
Peace, *quiet.*
Piece, *a part.*
Peer, *a nobleman.*
Pier, *a column.*

1

Place, *situation.*
Plaice, *a fish.*
Pray, *to beseech.*
Prey, *plunder.*
Plate, *a dish.*
Plait, *a fold.*
Raze, *to demolish.*
Raise, *to lift up.*
Rays, *sunbeams.*
Rain, *water from clouds.*
Reign, *to rule.*
Rein, *part of a bridle.*
Rye, *corn.*
Wry, *crooked.*
Rite, *a ceremony.*
Write, *to use a pen.*
Wright, *an artificer.*
Sale, *selling.*
Sail, *part of a ship.*
Seen, *beheld.*
Scene, *part of a play.*
See, *to behold.*
Sea, *the ocean.*
So, *thus.*
Sow, *to scatter abroad*
Sew, *to use a needle.*
Slight, *to despise.*
Sleight, *dexterity.*
Slow, *tardy.*
Sloe, *a fruit.*
Sole, *bottom of the foot.*
Soul, *the spirit of man.*
Sore, *an ulcer.*
Soar, *to fly aloft.*

1	2	3	4	1	2	1	2	1	2

fate, far, fall, fat,—me, met,—pine, pin,—no, move

1

Steel, *hardened iron.*
Steal, *to pilfer.*
Stile, *steps to a field.*
Style, *language.*
Strait, *narrow.*
Straight, *not crooked.*
Tale, *a story.*
Tail, *the end.*
Slay, *to kill.*
Sleigh, *a vehicle.*
Toe, *part of the foot.*
Tow, *coarse linen.*
Vale, *a velley.*
Veil, *a cover.*
Vane, *a weather cock.*
Vain, *worthless.*
Vein, *a blood vessel.*
Waste, *loss.*
Waist, *of the body.*
Week, *seven days.*
Weak, *not strong.*
You, *yourself.*
Yew, *a tree.*

2

Ark, *a vessel.*
Arc, *part of a circle.*
Bin, *a place for corn.*
Been, *participle of* to be.
Bell, *instrument of sound.*
Belle, *a young lady.*
But, *a conjunction.*
Butt, *a large cask.*
Bred, *brought up.*
Bread, *food.*

2

Sell, *to dispose of.*
Cell, *a pit or cave.*
Gilt, *with gold.*
Guilt, *sin.*
Herd, *a drove.*
Heard, *did hear.*
Him, *that man.*
Hymn, *a sacred song.*
Hart, *an animal.*
Heart, *seat of life.*
In, *within.*
Inn, *a public house.*
Kill, *to destroy life.*
Kiln, *for burning brick.*
Led, *did lead.*
Lead, *metal.*
Plum, *a fruit.*
Plumb, *a leaden weight.*
Ring, *a circle.*
Wring, *to twist.*
Rest, *repose.*
Wrest, *to force.*
Rung, *did ring.*
Wrung, *twisted.*
Ruff, *a ruffle.*
Rough, *uneven.*
Sent, *did send.*
Cent, *a copper corn.*
Sum, *the whole.*
Some, *a part.*
Sun, *source of light.*
Son, *a male child.*
Too, *likewise.*
Two, *twice one.*

3 4   1   2   3   32   33
nor, good,—tube, tub, bull,—oil, pound,—thin, THIS

3

All, *everyone.*
Awl, *an instrument.*
  Aught, *anything.*
  Ought, *bound by duty.*
Ball, *a round body.*
Bawl, *to cry aloud.*
  Call, *to name.*
  Caul, *part of an animal.*
Cord, *a small rope.*
Chord, *a right line.*
  Hall, *a large room.*
  Haul, *to pull.*
Naught, *bad.*
Nought, *nothing.*

4

  Cask, *a barrel.*
  Casque, *armor for the head.*
Dam, *mother of brutes.*
Damn, *to condemn.*
  Jam, *a conserve.*
  Jamb, *post of a door.*
Rap, *a smart blow.*
Wrap, *to fold together.*
  Tax, *a rate.*
  Tacks, *small nails.*

33

Bow, *to bend.*
Bough, *a branch.*

33

Flour, *fine meal.*
Flow-er, *blossom of plants.*
Foul, *filthy.*
Fowl, *a bird.*

2

  Ber' ry, *a small fruit.*
  Bu ry, *to inter.*
Les sen, *to make less.*
Les son, *a precept.*
  Suck er, *a small twig.*
  Suc cor, *help.*
Sel ler, *one who sells.*
Cel lar, *room under a house.*
  Cous in, *a relation.*
  Coz en, *to cheat.*
Sig net, *to seal.*
Cyg net, *a young swan.*
  Pen sile, *hanging.*
  Pen cil, *a small brush.*
Rig or, *severity.*
Rig ger, *a mechanic.*

1

  Seal' ing, *fixing a seal.*
  Ceil ing, *of a room.*
Vi ol, *an instrument.*
Vi al, *a small bottle.*

3

Al' ter, *to change.*
Al tar, *a place for sacrifice.*

1	2	3	4		1	2		1	2		1	2

fate, far, fall, fat,—me, met,—pine, pin,—no, move

SECTION XXXVIII.

Figures and Numbers.

Arabic.	Roman.	Names.	Numeral Adjectives.
1	I	One	First
2	II	Two	Second
3	III	Three	Third
4	IV	Four	Fourth
5	V	Five	Fifth
6	VI	Six	Sixth
7	VII	Seven	Seventh
8	VIII	Eight	Eighth
9	IX	Nine	Ninth
10	X	Ten	Tenth
11	XI	Eleven	Eleventh
12	XII	Twelve	Twelfth
13	XIII	Thirteen	Thirteenth
14	XIV	Fourteen	Fourteenth
15	XV	Fifteen	Fifteenth
16	XVI	Sixteen	Sixteenth
17	XVII	Seventeen	Seventeenth
18	XVIII	Eighteen	Eighteenth
19	XIX	Nineteen	Nineteenth
20	XX	Twenty	Twentieth
30	XXX	Thirty	Thirtieth
40	XL	Forty	Fortieth
50	L	Fifty	Fiftieth
60	LX	Sixty	Sixtieth
70	LXX	Seventy	Seventieth
80	LXXX	Eighty	Eightieth
90	XC	Ninety	Ninetieth
100	C	One hundred	One hundredth
500	D	Five hundred	Five hundredth
1000	M	One thousand	One thousandth

SECTION XXXIX.

Abbreviations used in Writing and Printing.

A. B. *Bachelor of Arts.*
A. A. S. *Fellow of the American Academy.*
A. D. *In the year of our Lord.*
A. M. *Master of Arts.*
A. M. *Before Noon.*
B. D. *Bachelor of Divinity.*
B. V. *Blessed Virgin.*
C. S. *Keeper of the Seal.*
D. D. *Doctor of Divinity.*
F. R. S. *Fellow of Royal Society.*
G. R. *George the King.*
H. B. M. *His Brittanic Majesty.*
K. *King.*
LL. D. *Doctor of Laws.*
L. S. *Place of the Seal.*
M. *Marquis.*
M. B. *Bachelor of Physic.*
MS. *Manuscript.*
MSS. *Manuscripts.*
N. B. *Take Notice.*
N. C. *North Carolina.*
N. H. *New Hampshire.*
N. J. *New Jersey*
N. S. *New Style.*
N. W. T. *North-West Territory.*
N. Y. *New York.*
O. S. *Old Style.*

P. M. *Post Master; Afternoon.*
P. O. *Post Office.*
P. S. *Postscript.*
Q. *Queen; Question.*
R. *The King.*
R. I. *Rhode Island.*
S. C. *South Carolina.*
S. T. D. *Doctor of Divinity*
U. S. A. *United States of America.*
Abp. *Archbishop.*
Acct. *Account.*
Ala. *Alabama.*
Apr. *April*
Att'y. *Attorney.*
Aug. *August.*
Bart. *Baronet.*
Capt. *Captain.*
Chap. *Chapter.*
Co. *Company.*
Col. *Colonel.*
Con. *On the other hand.*
Conn. *Connecticut.*
Cr. *Credit; Creditor.*
Cts. *Cents.*
Cwt. *Hundred weight.*
Dea. *Deacon.*
Dec. *December.*
Del. *Delaware.*
Dept. *Deputy.*
Do. *The same.*

Ditto. *The same.*
Dr. *Doctor; Debtor.*
Ed. *Edition; Editor.*
Eph. *Ephesians.*
Esa. *Esaias.*
Eccl. *Ecclesiastes.*
Eng. *England; English.*
Ep. *Epistle.*
Esq. *Esquire.*
Ex. *Example.*
Exr. *Executor.*
Feb. *February.*
Fr. *France; Francis.*
Gen. *General.*
Gent. *Gentlemen.*
Geo. *Georgia; George.*
Gov. *Governor.*
hhd. *Hogshead.*
Heb. *Hebrews.*
Hon. *Honorable.*
hund. *Hundred.*
Ibid. *The same.*
i. e. *That is.*
id. *The same.*
Ind. *Indiana.*
Inst. *Present.*
Isa. *Isaiah.*
Jan. January
Km. *Kingdom.*
Kt. *Knight*
Lat. *Latitude.*
Ld. *Lord.*
Ldp. *Lordship.*
lb. *Pound.*
Lieut. *Lieutenant.*

Lon. *Longitude.*
Lou. *Louisiana.*
Maj. *Major.*
Mar. *March.*
Mass. *Massachusetts.*
Math. *Mathematics.*
Md. *Maryland.*
Me. *Maine.*
Matt. *Matthew.*
Mr. *Master.*
Mrs. *Mistress.*
Messrs. *Gentlemen.*
No. *Number.*
Nov. *November.*
Obj. *Objection.*
Obt. *Obedient.*
Oct. *October.*
Parl. *Parliament.*
Penn. *Pennsylvania.*
per. *By.*
per cent. *By the Hundred.*
Pres. *President.*
Prof. *Professor.*
Ps. *Psalms.*
Regr. *Register.*
Rep. *Representative.*
Rev. *Reverend.*
Rt. Hon. *Right Honorable.*
St. *Saint.*
Sect. *Section.*
Sen. *Senator.*
Sept. *September.*
Servt. *Servant.*
ss. *To wit, namely.*
Tenn. *Tennessee.*

Thos. *Thomas.*	wt. *Weight.*
ult. *The last.*	yd. *Yard.*
Va. *Virginia.*	&, *And.*
Viz. *Namely.*	&c. *And the rest.*
Vt. *Vermont.*	vs. *against.*

SECTION XL.
Punctuation.

Punctuation is the art of dividing a written composition into sentences, or parts of sentences, by points or stops, to mark the different pauses which the sense requires.

The principal points are the

Comma thus	,	Interrogation, thus	?
Semicolon,	;	Exclamation,	!
Colon,	:	Parenthesis,	()
Period,	.	Dash,	—

A Comma denotes a pause as long as the reader would be in pronouncing the word *and*, or any other monosyllable in the sentence.

A Semicolon denotes a pause as long as two commas.

A Colon denotes a pause as long as three commas.

A Period denotes a pause as long as four commas: it shows that the sentence is complete.

An Interrogation Point denotes that a question is asked.

An Exclamation Point denotes astonishment, or some other emotion.

A Parenthesis includes a part of a sentence, which might have been omitted without injuring the sense, and must be read in an altered and lower tone of voice.

A Dash denotes a sudden stop, or change in the subject, and requires a pause longer than the period.

The following characters are also frequently used in composition:

An Apostrophe, thus ' denotes the omission of a letter; as *lov'd* for *loved*.

A Caret, thus v denotes where to take in what was left out by mistake; as thus, gram^mar

A Hyphen, thus - connects the parts of a compound word; as *lap-dog*. It is placed at the end of a line, when a word is divided, and one or more syllables put in the following line. When over a vowel, it denotes a long sound.

The Acute Accent thus ' as, *hon'-est.*

A Breve, thus ᵕ denotes the short sound of the vowel.

A Diaeresis, thus ¨ denotes that the vowel, over which it is placed, is not connected in sound with the foregoing vowel.

A Quotation, thus " " denotes that the passage is taken from some other author, in his own words.

An Index, thus ☞ points to a passage important to be noticed.

A Paragraph, thus ¶ denotes the beginning of a new subject.

A Star, thus * and other marks, as †, ‡, §, ||, and sometimes the letters of the alphabet, and figures, refer to the margin or bottom of the page.

CAPITAL LETTERS.

Capital letters should be used,

1. At the beginning of every book, chapter, note, and sentence.

2. At the beginning of appellations of the Deity; of proper names of persons, places, seas, rivers, ships; and of adjectives derived from proper names.

3. At the beginning of most quotations; of every line of poetry; and of some important word in a sentence.

APPENDIX.

The defective articulation which characterizes most readers and speakers of the present day, no doubt originates in the pupil's inattention whilst he is learning to spell. This defect consists principally, in want of distinctness in enunciating the vowel sounds of unemphatic words or syllables, and in neglecting to sound all but the last consonant, where two or more come together, at the end of a word.

Let the teacher attend closely to the reading on one of his classes, and he will find *constitution* almost invariably pronounced *const'ution*; *veracity* shortened into *verac'ty*; *nests* smoothed into *ness*, and so of all similar words. The conjunctions *and*, *that*, *if*, &c. either lose their vowel entirely, or have *u* short substituted for it. These defects can only be avoided by great care at a very early stage of the pupil's education. If a faulty articulation becomes fixed while the learner is spelling, it will be almost impossible to correct it entirely, no matter how great care be subsequently bestowed upon it.

With a view to assist the teacher, a few tables and exercises are subjoined, merely as models, which may be extended as far as may be found necessary; and to which the learner should be introduced as early as practicable—even before he knows the alphabet. Nor should he be permitted to pass over any lesson, until he is able to utter with facility, every sound contained in it, whether vowel or consonant.

TABLE OF THE VOWEL ELEMENTS.

In this table, the attention must be directed to the elementary *sounds*, actually heard in the words placed opposite to the letters, and not to the *names* of the letters. The same *letter* sometimes stands in different words for several *sounds*. The element is separated from the rest of the word by a hyphen, and is printed in *italics*. Let the teacher pronounce the word, then the element separately, and require each member of the class to do the same until perfect accuracy is attained. Care must be taken that the sound is full and clear, without any undue prolongation or drawl. It must begin and end abruptly, being as it were *coughed out.*

In thus exploding the vowels, the sound should be a pure *vocality*, unmixed with the aspirate.

1	e	as heard in	*e*-rr		9	ou	as heard in	*ou*-r
2	a	" " "	*a*-ll		10	ee	" " "	*ee*-l
3	o	" " "	*o*-r		11	i	" " "	*i*-t
4	a	" " "	*a*-ge		12	oo	" " "	*oo*-ze
5	e	" " "	*e*-dge		13	u	" " "	*pu*-ll
6	a	" " "	*a*-rm		14	oi	" " "	b-*oy*
7	*a*	" " "	*a*-t		15	i	" " "	*i*-sle
8	o	" " "	*o*-ld					

The following sentences contain words which are most commonly mutilated in pronunciation. Thus the following sentence, "The constitution and character that he had enjoyed were both ruined"—would generally be read "Th' cons'tution 'nd char'cter th't he'd 'njoyed w'r both ru'nd." The object of this table is to correct that fault.

(The letters in *italics* are those most likely to be dropped.)

These things are sim*i*lar.

Study, th*a*t *y*ou may *i*mprove.

James *a*nd John read po*e*try.
Your cur*i*os*i*ty is very great.
He *i*s a man of verac*i*ty.
His capac*i*ty is very great.
George is a po*e*t.
Have you seen the Gen*e*ral?
The town was fort*i*fied.
He depos*i*ted his money in the bank.
What quant*i*ty did he receive?
The fields pr*o*duce *a*bund*a*ntly.
His simplic*i*ty will be his ru*i*n.
We *a*re fond of po*e*try.
He reads Lat*i*n.
Hist*o*ry *i*s a prof*i*table study.
He w*a*s driv*e*n by n*e*cess*i*ty.
Be temp*e*rate.
The cons*e*quences will be ru*i*nous.
That is imposs*i*ble.
What vivac*i*ty!
The Omnip*o*tent Be*i*ng.
The cont*i*nent of *A*merica.
The only poss*i*bil*i*ty.
He heard the rec*i*tation.
The cause of temp*e*rance.
He has held sev*e*ral off*i*ces.
Avoid quarr*e*ls.
Advers*i*ty tries friends.
He *a*pplied to the gov*e*ror.
The case is sing*u*lar.
Has he been *a*ppointed?

The teacher may pronounce these and similar sentences, requiring each individual of the class to repeat the same words, taking care that in the *distinct* pronunciation of the italicized vowels, the pupil does not fall into the opposite fault of giving them undue emphasis.

CONSONANT ELEMENTS AND
THEIR COMBINATIONS.

Each consonant requires a different position of the organs of speech. If the vowel *a* as heard in the syllable *at*, be placed before B, P and M; and the syllables thus formed be slowly pronounced, the position of the organs, and the method of giving precision and force to the consonant elements, will thus become apparent. The same exercise upon the other consonants will give *their* power also.

Although the consonant elements cannot be uttered with as much distinctness as the vowels, yet they are capable of a considerable degree of it; and a distinct articulation requires a vigorous utterance of the consonants as well as of the vowels.

In the table of consonant elements, the same care must be taken, as in the case of the vowels, to separate the power or sound of the consonant, or consonants as heard in the word from the name of the letters. Let the word be pronounced slowly, in order that the distinct sound may be observed, and then let that sound be uttered alone. The teacher should not be discouraged at the seeming inability of young pupils to follow him in this exercise; as practice will soon remove every difficulty.

1 b	as heard in	*b*-old	8 n	as heard in	*n*-ot
2 d	" " "	*d*-ay	9 q	" " "	*q*-uit
3 f	" " "	*f*-ine	10 r	" " "	*r*-ot
4 g	" " "	*g*-ap	11 v	" " "	*v*-ine
5 j	" " "	*j*-oy	12 w	" " "	*w*-ay
6 l	" " "	*l*-ine	13 y	" " "	*y*-oke
7 m	" " "	*m*-at	14 z	" " "	*z*-one

After sufficient practice upon the preceding table, the pupil may be required to pronounce *combinations* of these elements, such as the teacher may think fit. Underneath is a table, containing some of the most difficult, as they occur in common words.*

rb	as in	o-*rb*	rm	as in	a-*rm*
br	" "	*br*-and	rn	" "	bu-*rn*
bs	" "	ri-*bs*	rp	" "	ha-*rp*
bz	" "	pro-*bes*	rt	" "	hea-*rt*
dr	" "	*dr*-ove	rv	" "	cu-*rve*
ds	" "	dee-*ds*	rz	" "	e-*rrs*
fl	" "	*fl*-ame	rsh	" "	ha-*rsh*
fs	" "	cli-*ffs*	rth	" "	ea-*rth*
gr	" "	*gr*-ave	sh	" "	*sh*-ip
gs	" "	pi-*gs*	sk	" "	ma-*sk*
kr	" "	*cr*-ony	sl	" "	*sl*-ay
ks	" "	thin-*ks*	sm	" "	*sm*-oke
ld	" "	ho-*ld*	sn	" "	*sn*-ail
lb	" "	bu-*lb*	sp	" "	*sp*-it
lp	" "	he-*lp*	st	" "	*st*-arve
ls	" "	fa-*lse*	str	" "	*str*-ong
lt	" "	fe-*lt*	sts	" "	bu-*sts*
md	" "	ento-*mb'd*	th	" "	*th*-istle
mf	" "	hu-*mph*-ry	thm	" "	ry-*thm*
mt	" "	atte-*mpt*	tr	" "	*tr*-ap
nt	" "	se-*nt*	tz	" "	ha-*ts*
ns	" "	fi-*ns*	vn	" "	dri-*ven*
pl	" "	*pl*-uck	zm	" "	spa-*sm*
pr	" "	*pr*-ay	zms	" "	spa-*sms*
rj	" "	ba-*rge*	sts	" "	ne-*sts*
rf	" "	su-*rf*	dths	" "	brea-*dths*
rk	" "	ha-*rk*	ftst	" "	wa-*ft'st*
rl	" "	sna-*rl*	nkst	" "	thi-*nkst*

* See Barber's Grammar of Elocution.

lsht	as in	fi-*lch'd*	vst	as in	li-*v'st*
skst	" "	ma-*sk'st*	lpst	" "	he-*lpst*
znst	" "	impri-*sons't*	shr	" "	*shr*-ub

The pupil may next be required to pronounce after his teacher, the following or similar sentences, giving particular attention to the articulation of the conso-nent element.

He reached the bird's nests.
She acts strangely.
She mixed the colors.
Threads of the same length.
What gifts are these?
The depths of the sea.
I crushed the wretch.
What fear'st thou?
His attempts were vain.
She holds his hands.
What are his wants?
Earth's ample breasts.
It hurts me.
He bursts away.
We have hearts.
See these shrubs.
They wagged their heads.
Six cubits in height.
He was the sixth son.
She has three assistants.
The cats sleep on the rug.
Here are two baskets.

By faithful practice upon such exercises as the forgoing the pupil will soon acquire a distinct and proper articulation, the foundation of excellence in both speaking and reading.